Deborah Burnett ASID

Comfortable Living by *Design*

Down-to-Earth Decorating Advice for a Warm and Friendly Home

HUMBLE
ABUNDANCE
PUBLISHING

Published by

Humble Abundance Publishers
140 Old Kinneys School Rd.
Springfield, TN 37172

phone: 615/384-8337
fax: 615/384-1137
email: dawb@mindspring.com

Cover design: Mary Caprio
Book design: Michelle White
Photography: Mark Martin

Printed in the United States of America

ISBN 0-9672167-0-2

Hello and Welcome,

Since this book is a new literary approach to the subject of decorating and design, we'd love hearing your comments and would appreciate you sharing your project success stories with us.

Don't be bashful ... send negative comments as well, because I've always looked at *lemons* as a great way to improve on the next batch of *lemonade*! So feel free to visit our website, drop us a note, or call ...we'll be looking forward to hearing from you.

Debra

Humble Abundance Publishers
140 Old Kinneys School Road
Springfield, TN 37172

phone: (800) 265-2992
fax: (615) 384-1137
email: dawb@mindspring.com
website: www.deborahburnett.com

TABLE OF CONTENTS

To those angels who've guided,
prodded and directed me
while seeking the truth in who I am –
many thanks!

INTRODUCTION

*W*hile writing my first book, *The Adventures of RICHIE RICH* (Third Grade Publishers, 1961) I learned a valuable lesson – too bad I didn't remember it while writing this book.

Back then, writing was a school assignment that had to be completed within a given time frame. So between play yard activities, Barbie-doll imaginary parties and army with the boys – I know, I can't help it, I was a tomboy – I found time to express my thoughts on paper. That little spoiled rich kid, RICHIE RICH, gave me an outlet to have creative fun while completing a school assignment. Little did I know that I would eventually work on the *book* long after the assignment due date.

My teacher, Ms. Thumb, encouraged me to take my time and develop my thoughts clearly, as if I were painting pictures with my words. When I finished with my 26 page masterpiece, I felt a sense of accomplishment, and then went on to other activities. If I remember clearly, by that time, I was *into* designing the family underground bomb shelter (I've always said that my construction and design background really does go *way* back!) Anyway, the lesson I learned was that once I had completed my thoughts, applied them to the gray lined paper, and then stapled the pages into the red cover, I was *finished*!

Unfortunately, in 1999, while writing this book, I realized that same sense of "finished" will not be possible; there is just too much information I'd like to share and I simply don't have the time or page count to complete those additional thoughts. So for now, consider this book a unique and most unusual literary approach to decorating and design - the first in a series of books that will attempt to "teach" rather than show the art and skill of decorating.

Throughout *Comfortable Living by Design*, you'll notice that the arrangement of the chapters and contents are somewhat jumbled, but with a *touch* of organization. This I did on purpose to force you to look at decorating with *new eyes*. The content, style and lack of photographs is also different from other decorating books currently on the market today. This, too, was designed to force you to consider the actual skill of decorating with a new sense of appreciation.

Finally, the design principles and elements covered within these too few pages were purposely chosen so that you can begin to understand decorating and design in a whole new light. And it's that new light of understanding that I hope will create in you a deeper awareness of your God-given skill of creativity so that you, too, can design *your* home comfortably.

Deborah Burnett
July, 1999

chapter one

LET THERE BE LIGHT
The Key Element for a Warm and Friendly Home

*P*racticing interior design for the past 20 years, I can honestly say that I've heard the following request thousands of times: "I want it to be light and airy, comfortable and reasonably fashionable, and, of course, on a budget." I shake my head and chuckle. It doesn't seem to make any difference whether the residential client is contemporary or hard-core colonial, the request is always the same. They all want a comfortable home that is warm and friendly – a home that is designed to impart a feeling of relaxation and contentment, one which will evoke pleasurable feelings from all who enter.

For some, that desired decorating style is sleek and elegant with a wonderfully restrained use of color. Others are more at ease living with darker colors, lots of interesting textures and being surrounded with natural woodtones. Still others just love mixing several styles and letting their personalities tie it all together. But no matter what their style requests have been, I have found that the *design* solution to achieving a comfortable home is simple – all I need to do is add *light*.

A few winters ago, I had the opportunity to be walking on the Vanderbilt University campus during a rare Spring-like afternoon. The January sky was crystal blue and the air was unseasonably sweet with the smell of an early growth. But the most amazing aspect of that memorable afternoon was the light.

It was so clear and intense that it made all of the surrounding natural colors seem to "pop" to life. Looking about, I noticed that even the exposed bark of the bare-leafed trees had been transformed into a wonderful mottled gray highlighted with flecks of tobacco brown. And it seemed that all of nature's colors contained within the winter campus were also vibrant and alive.

> "And God said, 'Let there be lights in the firmament of the heaven to divide the day from the night; and let them be for signs, and for seasons, and for days and years'."
> — Genesis 1:14

And it wasn't just me who noticed. Every one of the passing students seemed to have an accompanying smile to their wandering eyes as they searched the tree tops for signs of the approaching early spring. In other words, everyone was pleasantly surprised by the unusual natural light and warm weather conditions. It made them smile unconsciously and added a bounce to their steps. Just being in that wonderful outdoor environment was a tonic to the winter-weary spirit of everyone I passed.

As a trained professional interior designer who knows the benefits of natural light, I was not surprised by the students' reaction; I had seen it before. I couldn't help but recall that same *"unconscious smile"* on every one of my clients faces who have walked into a recently remodeled or constructed house detailed with spacious windows and multiple

> **Natural light is so important in not only what and how we "see" but also in how we "feel" about our environment.**

skylights. The common bond between the students and my clients? *Light* – both situations were flooded with natural light.

So every time I see this *"unconscious smile"* reaction I'm reminded of a houseplant bending and straining towards the nearest window to gain more light. And no wonder – it's the *light* that causes the feeling of well-being. It's the *light* that makes us feel good. When you think about it, humans

The design solution to achieving a comfortable home is simple – all I need to do is add light.

and plants are all striving to feel better about their space, and the use of God's light is a wonderful catalyst to achieve that comfortable feeling.

*N*atural light. It sounds so simple and basic, but it's so important in not only what and how we "see" but also in how we *feel* about our environment. So what does this have to do with decorating? Everything!

Especially when you consider that most modern homes today are small box-like structures with randomly placed windows on the vertical walls – in other words, no opportunity for an abundance of natural light to stream in from above. Wait a minute … light comes from above. Hmm – something look out of order here?

> **Natural light fills the human spirit with that all important sense of vitality and comfort.**

Okay, the small box-like structure part is accurate, but the practice of placing the window openings on the vertical side walls instead of the roofline seems to be in contradiction with the natural order of light. When you think about it, why *is* the window on the wall instead of on the roof if the whole purpose is to let in natural light?

Now, don't get me wrong. I'm not questioning current building practice. Wall windows *do* serve an important purpose by allowing the occupants to view the outside, and offering a means of secondary escape in case of fire. And wall windows also

In order to make a room more comfortable be sure to add lots of different sources of light.

add an architectural element to an otherwise blank wall. But if you consider roof windows – now there's the answer if you want to allow natural light to flood an interior space *and* to fill the human spirit with that all important sense of vitality and comfort.

Come again? *Light gives comfort?* Hey – if you're having trouble understanding this thought, go ahead and think back to the last time you went into a basement or back storeroom. Didn't you automatically "know" that you were far from the natural source of light just by the feeling of that subterranean space? Your skin and other sensory organs could tell that you were in a basement or non-windowed back room, even if you were blindfolded, because your internal "comfort level" automatically changed.

When we humans are deprived of natural light we actually feel it. And if we can *feel* this light level change, does it not make sense that light is the key ingredient to a room when we are trying to make it *feel* comfortable? Since natural light is not always available, doesn't it also make sense to increase the amount of artificial light present within the room in order to make up for the lost natural light? Hey – could be we're on to something here! So if a great room with a warm and friendly *feeling* is what you are after, then in order to make a

> "My darkness has been filled with the light of intelligence."
> – Helen Keller

room more comfortable, be sure to add *lots* of light: uplights, mood lights, portrait lights, table lamps, recessed lights, and any other source of light.

So back to the question of why roof windows or skylights are not the norm if the whole purpose of windows is to let in light? The answer is simple. It's *easier* to install a window than a skylight, which translates to fewer $$$ for the overall cost of the house.

Let's face it. In standard residential construction markets, builders are usually not aware of the benefits of natural light and are concerned only with the bottom line cost of the house. Thus, the majority of homes today do not feature skylights. So, as a

> **With a little understanding ... you will be able to achieve the correct balance of light.**

homeowner or apartment dweller where the only source of natural light is from a few undersized windows, what's the answer? Well, don't panic. With a little understanding of the three basic types of light, you will be able to achieve the correct balance of light in order to feel comfortable in your own home – without having to install lots of skylights.

$\mathcal{T}$o help you better understand light, here's a brief explanation of the three types of light necessary for a successful decorating/design project.

KINETIC LIGHT – This is any light source where you can actually feel, see, or sense heat and movement in addition to the light. The inviting glow and heat from an open fireplace or the flickering flame from a beeswax candle all give light *and* impart a physical sense of warmth and vitality to the overall temperature of the room. So, whenever a woman wants to set a romantic mood, is it any wonder that she tends to light a candle and turn off the overheads?

· **Candles**
· **Lanterns**
· **Fireplace**
· **Wood Stove**

And when you think about it, it's the actual warmth and feeling of the light that "charges our batteries" and puts us in a relaxed mood.

NATURAL LIGHT – God's gift of light, which is provided by the sun, moon, stars, dawn and other natural occurrences, are all so necessary to enable our lives to thrive.

· **Sun**
· **Stars**
· **Lightning**
· **Dusk**

Without even the tiniest bit of natural light we cannot function or even exist. So how can we expect our homes to feel comfortable if we don't even provide at least one window or glassed opening to the outside?

❧ *ARTIFICIAL LIGHT* – Any light produced by electricity or gas with a light source of either incandescent (regular light bulb) or energy-saving fluorescent is classified as artificial. We further divide this class into two groups:

• *ARCHITECTURAL* - Any light source that is constructed into or becomes a part of the building. Recessed light fixtures are a good example of the way to spread an even glow of light throughout an entire room.

· **Track Lighting**
· **Cove Lighting**

• *DECORATIVE* – Any light source that is portable or easily removed from the building. Regular table lamps and plant uplights are the perfect answer to fill a dark and dreary space with a warm glow of light.

· **Floor Lamps**
· **Buffet Lamps**

Now that you know about the importance of light, before you start your next decorating or design project, be sure to keep in mind (and include) the three types of light in each and every room. With a balanced lighting plan for each room, your finished decorating project will not only be seen but actually *felt* to be truly comfortable. So as a final reminder, be sure to:

- include 3 table lamps in every room
- provide at least 1 window for every 100 square feet of floor space
- include 1 uplight behind every plant over 4' tall.

**... Still unsure about using light correctly?
Don't hesitate to drop us a
line with questions.**

DESIGN BASICS ...

Whenever using a torchier floor lamp, be sure to insert a pastel peach bulb instead of a regular 60 watt white bulb in order to give extra impact to an otherwise dull ceiling. These peach or light pink bulbs are a good idea because they give a soft and comfortable look to the overall living space. These bulbs are also wonderful to use in your overhead bedroom fixtures especially if you're over 40 – the soft pinkish peach light is fantastic for hiding facial lines and wrinkles.

Replace ceiling fixture bulbs with an IQ DIMMER BULB. They sell for under $5.00 and take the place of an electrically installed dimmer device. When you need lots of light flip once for 100 watts or three more times to get a nice cozy light down to 20 watts.

Want to update an old lamp without spending a lot of money? For under $50.00 you can change the harp to the next smallest size, add a black paper shade and tie a drapery chair tassel around the throat. WOW! What a difference!

Install track or recessed accent lights around the perimeter of the room. Mount them approximately 3 feet from the wall and be sure to paint the track head or the cans' trim the same color of the ceiling so as not to be so noticeable. If the ceiling height is over 16 feet, use a **PAR** type of bulb. For standard 8 foot ceilings try the new **ER** series. It will save on energy costs!

Use uplights behind large plants and accent furniture to lighten up the corners of the room. Since these luminaries are constantly turned on and are subject to get extremely hot, I recommend the use of the new compact fluorescent instead of the incandescent 40 watt. The Phillips #**SLS 15** will give a nice warm glow instead of the usual greenish glare you'd expect from a regular fluorescent.

Time to change the fluorescent tubes in your bath or kitchen? Why not consider installing a fluorescent tube with a **3500 KELVIN** temperature rating (3500K) so that your skin will no longer have that horrible green

or orange glow? The lighting from these specialty tubes will actually make your skin and
clothes look more true to life plus have the
added benefit of actually lasting longer
between changes.

The bright light from the new tabletop
halogen lamps is perfect for use on desks and
other work areas. But when it comes to
changing the bulb, extra care needs to be
taken. Be sure not to touch the surface of the
replacement bulb; the oil from your skin will
cause the bulb to burst and could cause injury
from flying glass. SAFETY TIP: always wear
gloves or cover your fingers with a plastic bag
whenever handling the bare bulb.

Lamp shades are a great way to add personality to an otherwise dull lamp base. For
professional results, why not try adding a
black paper shade in a "coolie" design? The
sharply sloped shade form adds dramatic
interest as well as directs the light downward
for a classic look. Even if the lamp base is tra-

ditional, don't be afraid to experiment with the coolie shape - you'll love the results!

Using candles is a great way to add a touch of romantic comfort to our lives, but whenever actually lighting and enjoying the flickering candles be sure to keep these safety tips in mind:

· Trim the wicks to 1/4 inch after each and every burn session - this will help maintain the appearance as well as the potential flammability of the actual candle.

· Never leave candles burning while not in the room. It's just like a small infant ... you never know what could happen. So why take the chance?

Cleaning the actual light bulb as well as the fixture is not only a housekeeping necessity, but will save you money as well. Recent studies have shown that as much as 80% of the energy used to produce light from an ordinary lightbulb is wasted due to an accumulation of dust and other dirt particulates on the surface of the glass bulb. So for better light and a few less wasted dollars, be sure to get out the dust rag for the **TOP** of the bulb as well as the shade and base.

For new construction projects be sure to specify the use of recessed light fixtures throughout the entire house. They not only afford better lighting patterns but actually can cost less money when compared to the highly decorative surface-mounted styles. The installation may be more costly, but you should consider the savings over typical ceiling-mounted fixtures, plus the fact that you won't have to make another design statement in a few years (which, by the way, **WILL** change). The answer is simple - recessed lighting is the best way to light the way through your new home!

Whenever traipsing through flea markets, be on the lookout for old dining room-type chandeliers - they make great candle holders! All you have to do is simply remove the wiring and false socket sleeves where the light bulbs

usually mount and then position fat squatty
candles on each arm platform. Secure the candle with a dollop of "liquid nails" or other super-
strong adhesive, making sure it doesn't wobble
or have a chance to fall. Then just hoist the
entire fixture up to a ceiling hook and **WOW!** -
instant **OLD WORLD** lighting!

Design Notes ...

_____

_____

_____

_____

_____

_____

_____

_____

_____

_____

_____

_____

The secret for a successful design project?
Simple ... just add light!

chapter two

FROM HOUSE TO HOME
The Transforming Ingredient
is Comfort

*S*o many times, we've all had such grand "decorating" ideas planned for our homes that we tend to over-
look the basic needs of our nest. By that, I mean those
qualities and little touches that make our house our "true
home." You know, little things like a really comfortable
chair in which to relax while watching that favorite TV
show, or a well-lit and organized kitchen work area. And
let's not fail to mention a wonderfully inviting and peace-
ful atmosphere in our master bedrooms. All of those
attributes go into creating a comfortable home.

It's unfortunate, but a lot of D-I-Y (do-it-yourself) decorators tend to concentrate too long and hard on decorative items, such as accessories and furniture, and fail to recognize the most basic of all human home needs – comfort. Let's face it – without an attractive, clean and comfortable home environment how can we be expected to go out each morning and then feel glad to return each evening to the place we call home if it's *not* comfortable?

Since grade school, it seems that every few years I have developed a lapse of memory and taken on the challenge of participating in local theater. I don't know what it is about the performing arts that seems to have this pull on my common sense; maybe it's the vitality or excitement, or could be that I like not sleeping for six weeks (nah!). All I know is that every few years, I agree to become involved with the local theater group by helping with the sets for an upcoming production. Sometimes, I even get brave and take on an acting role.

Throughout my so-called performing career, I've been involved in everything from *The Diary of Anne Frank* to *Alice in Wonderland*. As varied as each of these productions have been, I've always found one constant – *impression* – the impression that I portray as an actor *or* the

> **"Without an attractive, clean comfortable place we call home, why bother?"**
> **– Deborah Burnett**

impression I give to the audience as set designer. And it's that *"instant impression"* the audience will have of the play's temperament which will determine how I, as a set designer, will arrange the stage for the actors to play out their roles.

My challenge then is to arrange the entire set for *immediate understanding* – from color choices, furniture style and placement, wall treatments, scrim design and usage, prop detail, etc. It's so important that the audience know – from the second the curtain rises – what the mood of that scene is about.

Years ago, while working on the set design for *Anne Frank*, the challenge was to make it obvious that times were hard but that love and care persisted throughout the home the actors inhabited. Wherever a chair was called for, I made sure it was worn but comfortably outfitted with a generous throw pillow and crocheted arm covers. For the cramped but inviting central gathering room where the

> It's so important that the audience know – from the second the curtain rises – what the mood of that scene is about.

actors portrayed the real-life victims, a close-together grouping of aged but oversized chairs and sofas dominated. The overall lighting was dim, but wherever Anne was supposed to write in her diary or any of the other actors scheduled to read or sew, I had to plan for lamps, candles, windows, or lanterns – the space had to be *immediately* recognizable by the audience as real and suitable for the task at hand.   I had to make it comfortable and believable for the actors to perform their given scene – otherwise the audience would not buy it.

> **Space has to be immediately recognizable as real and suitable for the task.**

For the play *Dracula*, a progressively evil, depressed and foreboding temperament was called for. The action was to take place over a bleak and dreary four week period, but never once in the script did the actors mention that timeline. My job was to convey that fact through set design.

To represent the drawing room of an unfriendly mansion, we used *undersized stiff-backed* seating without regard to the actors' physical statures. The lighting was harsh, casting great shadows while accentuating the pallor of the grey-white color scheme.

Nothing was comfortable about the set. To immediately demonstrate the passage of time and convey a sense of disregard, I relied on the use and placement of real plants and household debris.

For the first act, I had positioned several healthy live ferns throughout the set. Act Two brought about a swapping of these healthy ferns for ones that were wilted and in need of water. When the curtain rose on the third act, the ferns were totally dead and browned.

What better way to say that nobody cares than by leaving a dead plant in the room?

We just placed the dead ferns in the exact spot as the healthy ferns in Act One. What better way to say that nobody has cared for this home for a long time than by leaving a dead plant in the room?

As a further indicator of time spent in disregard to the well-being of the rooms, the undersized furniture all took on a layer of gray film to indicate dust. Scattered about the set were other indicators – torn and droopy draperies, overflowing ashtrays, and of course, books and newspapers scattered about.

By the third act, this unspoken passage of time had been successfully conveyed to the audience. The overall temperament of progressive disregard for human comfort was also immediately evident by the dirty and worn condition of the set. This negative impression was conveyed *instantly* by just letting the plants die, allowing the dust to collect, painting the wrong room colors for the lighting conditions, and by using inappropriately scaled and non-functional furnishings – everything a comfortable room is not!

> **"Man built the house but woman made it a home."**
> **– Emily Post**

Hey, wait a minute! If it's the case that just by paying attention to little decorating and design details an immediate impression can be made about the room and those folks who live there, could it be that the same set design tricks used to convey a play's temperament are also those needed to bring a comfortable atmosphere to our homes? You bet! And, more importantly, this same technique when used in our homes can be used *successfully* from the moment the front door is opened.

> ...could it be that the same set design tricks used to convey a play's temperament are also those needed to bring a comfortable atmosphere to our homes?

Just like audiences who instantly know the play's temperament by viewing the opening set design, with only a few well-placed and thought out design and decorating tips, our own homes can be instantly recognized and designed to be comfortable.

*T*o get you started working towards designing that perfect set for the play we'll call *Welcome to Our Comfortable Home,* here are a few pointers:

⟨⟩ *Turn on the music.* That's right, select a soft and soothing station or series of CDs and arrange the speakers so that music fills the air of your home on a constant and regular basis. It takes such little energy to operate modern sound systems that it should be of no great concern for you to leave it on –

> **"Music alone can bind the wandering sense and calm the troubled mind."**
> **– Confucius**

even while you're away. Just think how much more inviting it is to walk into a home that's filled with softly playing background music – even if you know no one is at home. An empty house doesn't have to feel lonely.

Arrange the lighting (table lamps, uplights, portrait lights, etc.) so that the light provided fills the space evenly and gives the correct amount of light for the task at hand. Sound confusing? Here are some basics: if you want to read by a table lamp, make sure it's taller than your shoulder while sitting, and that it gives off a soft but strong glow. And wherever you have a table or empty space on top of a chest or other piece of furniture that can accommodate a lamp, *use* it! The most truly comfortable homes all utilize numerous lamps to provide atmosphere, light and a sense of "home".

*S*ince the most important element of residential design – *comfort* – is so elusive, but necessary in turning a house into a true home, why not take the time to learn how to recognize *comfort* when you see it? Listed below are several great opportunities to look and learn!

- Visit local designer "Show Homes" to see the latest in style and color usage as well as a stylized version of comfort.

- Watch old black and white movies by paying attention to the set designer's skills that convey mood and drama – the '40s were a particularly great era!

- Pay attention to where your house pet naps – it's usually the most strategically positioned for viewing household activity as well as being the most *naturally* comfortable within your present design scheme.

DESIGN BASICS ...

Impressed by the designer-look of throw pillows lovingly arranged on a sofa? To keep them comfy, be sure to fluff and punch each pillow daily so that the down, filling and other fibers can breathe. By plumping the pillow it will remain soft and pliable and not become hard and over-inflated like an old basketball!

For a warm and inviting home, display loose potpourri in every room and be sure to replace it at least once every three months. Store the spent potpourri in a paper sack in a dark closet after adding a few drops of refresher oil to the mix. Wait three months and voila! – a fresh batch of potpourri can be used again to freshen your comfortable home!

Want to give your home that "comfy designer look"? It's easy. Just use hardback glossy jacketed books to decorate with! Collect lots of flat coffee table-size books featuring your color scheme in the cover photo and use the books under lamps, propped against the back of bookcases, and even under flower arrangements. Stacked on the floor beside a favorite chair is okay, too. See? It's easy to decorate like a pro!

Starting a paint project? Before you buy the paint, test the paint chip sample in the room during morning light, early evening light and artificial light from lamps, TVs and other sources. Don't be surprised if you see three different colors, so be sure to tell the paint clerk to lighten or darken the color formula accordingly prior to mixing so that you end up with a color suited to all three lighting conditions.

It seems that all the most comfortable looking rooms have at least one knotted and fringed throw draped over a comfy chair or tossed at the foot of a luxurious bed. So why does your's look like granny's folded shawl? Because you're trying too hard! Instead of folding and placing, just gather it in the center using your thumb and index finger and then just throw it like you would a dead mouse or dirty diaper. See, it's that easy to get a comfortable designer look!

Most folks make the mistake of packing potpourri into deep dark containers. This does not allow for air circulation, the necessary element that is needed to make your room smell nice from the crushed flowers and herbs. Try using only a small handful in wide-mouthed containers throughout the room. Every few days fluff & toss to revive the potpourri. In the winter months, stuff an old nylon stocking with fresh potpourri and lay it near a floor heat vent. The rising warm air will freshen your entire house!

Want to create a relaxing and comfortable home for yourself and family? Well, try a little soft music playing in the background of your home activities. The sounds of a soft instrumental or soothing melody can actually make your home feel more comfortable and inviting. Keep the volume down low so that you can still converse, watch TV and read comfortably. Remember, the music is BACKGROUND to your life so keep it softly quiet.

In homes where space is at a premium, it's **OKAY** to sell a piece of furniture. Why keep something if it's cluttering up your space? Why not give treasured family pieces to a newlywed family member or college student? They could actually use the furniture and not just keep it around to collect dust!

Ever wonder why throw pillows always end up on the floor instead of on the sofa? It's lack of comfort! Who wants to sit with a hard basketball-like pillow pushing against your lower back bone? Since most ready-made pillows consist of hard foam forms and tightly stretched face fabrics with little or no comfy detail such as fringe or decorative welts, it's no wonder that whenever you lean against this type of sofa pillow it's like snuggling up to a beach ball! On the other hand, down-filled throw pillows are so mushy and snuggly that actually sitting on the sofa with a throw pillow against your back is really **COMFORTABLE**, but unfortunately, these pillows are rather expensive.

So if you don't have the budget to opt for expensive designer down-filled custom throw pillows (average price is $120 per pillow), the next best thing is to remake the store-bought throw pillows to sit and look like the more expensive down-filled ones. Here's how: make a small 6 inch split in the upper seam of the pillow and reach into the bag to remove a few wads of the fiberfill stuffing. Usually enough to fit into a small purse is sufficient to get the right "mushy feel".

Remember, your goal is to have the fabric cover hanging loose on the fiberfill stuffing so that the pillow still has a form but it's now "mushy-looking". After sewing the seam back, finish it off by cinching an oversized tasseled drapery tie-back around the pillow.

For a comfortable looking bathroom, try adding a small piece of furniture to whatever floor space you have. A unique small-scale table works great tucked under a pedestal sink, especially when it's filled with baskets of wonderfully aromatic soaps and other bath goodies. For larger bathrooms, a bakers rack also helps to solve the storage problem by

allowing extra shelving to display oversized
baskets filled with bath towels and other products such as shampoo and conditioner bottles.

   To insure a comfy chair, especially when it
comes time to recover, be sure to request that
your upholsterer replaces **ALL** of the existing
cushions with new "quality grade" foam. Trying
to save a few dollars on this aspect of the job
is not a great idea and will only cost you $$$ in
the long run.

   Another tip to guarantee a great looking
(and sitting) chair is to have the shop actually
wrap the cushion in several layers of dacron
fiberfill. This added extra touch gives the look
of an expensive down-fill cushion instead of just
a foam cushion. See? A little touch can add a
better feel **AND** give the appearance of a more
costly upholstered piece.

When shopping for a mattress, dress comfortably for the outing. No dresses or tight slacks here; you need to lay down and sprawl out on each and every mattress you are considering. Think of it as a "test rest". Don't worry about what the salesman will think - he's seen it all before.

Now is not the time to get embarrassed. And most importantly, if you're sleeping with a partner, only consider a queen or king size mattress. Did you realize that a full or standard double-size bed crams both of you into the same sleeping space as only a crib-size mattress? Ouch!

And lastly, buy the most expensive set you can afford. Don't try to skimp by buying mismatched sets. Since most mattresses and box springs were designed to work together, selecting something other than a complete matched set just defeats the design and gives YOU a bad night's sleep!

Expand the development of
your decorating skills through my
"You Can Do It!" video series.
Call 1-800-265-2992 for details.

Design Notes ...

_____

_____

_____

_____

_____

_____

_____

_____

_____

_____

_____

_____

Home is nothing more than an extension of ourselves.

chapter
three

THE BIG PICTURE

**When Building and Remodeling,
Plan for a Comfortable End Result**

*S*o many times throughout the years, I've been for-
tunate to become involved with hundreds of people's
daily lives while they're in the process of trying to fulfill
their dreams ... in other words, they're in the middle of a
building project and I'm the professional trying to hold
them to original plans, budget or immediate problems at
hand – a big challenge especially when the client is his or
her own worst enemy. It seems everyone expects the project to "look" great *without regard* to budgeting for all of the
money necessary to pull it off in the style they expect. You
see, they fail to keep an eye towards achieving the *real* end

result of their remodeling and construction efforts – creating a comfortable place to live out their lives, a place to call home.

*H*oliday gatherings and parties are a great time to catch up on the "news" ... what's been happening with friends and acquaintances and other bits of gossip. For the past few years, it seems that at every party I've attended, an aging baby-boomer has announced the

> **"You don't go from zero to hero without working at it."**
> – Carol G. Anderson

blessed event; she is finally going to build that dream house or undergo an extensive remodeling project! When I hear those words, I am so pleased for my friend's good fortune, until I hear those unfortunate words ... "And of course it will be awhile before we can afford to furnish, do the draperies and other accessories."

My disappointment is not centered on potential business lost, but on the loss of common decorating sense on the part of my friend. My heart just sinks knowing that the end result my friend is expecting will not be realized, and that she will not become aware of this until it's too late.

Throughout my career, I've been sharing thoughts on everything from practical Christmas decorations to health reasons for closing and flushing the commode, so here goes ... my biggest and best piece of advice to those considering remodeling or building a new home: if you are middle-aged and planning to build a new home (or undertake an extensive remodel), *don't do it* – unless you can afford to do it right! Spending money on a new home is fine, but don't get carried away with the "bigger is better" square footage game and end up short on cash for the really important things that will make your new house a *true home*.

> "Remodeling budget-buster – saying these words to your contractor; 'While you're here...' "
> – Deborah Burnett

Face it, after 50, you don't have many years left to dream of that perfect sofa or other decorative item that will make your home life attractive and comfortable. Also, our changing bodily needs affect the way we actually *use* our square footage and the furnishings within.

Think I'm kidding? If you're over 40, how easy would it be for *you* to get out of a bean-bag chair? Also, consider the use of the space. Now that the kids are gone, why is it necessary to have a large bonus or play room?

When we consider that in our 20s and 30s families are in a growing mode, and they require more space, usually faster than the money is flowing in, it's acceptable to have an empty room or a house filled with mismatched, leftover, and worn furniture. But in

> **"Small steps can bring huge results."**
> – Carol G. Anderson

our mature years, we need to think and look towards the future and our *creature comforts* within the time we have left. And if we've been given the means to improve our lot, then we need to do it with an end result of *comfort* in mind.

So what makes our new home or remodeled areas within the existing residence comfortable? Of course it's those little architectural things that count, such as extra construction upgrades in moldings, cabinets, flooring selections and other options that you may enjoy. But what makes up our true day-to-day comfortable feeling within a new home? Unfortunately, it's those items that most folks never seem to be able to afford because they've spent all the available funds actually building the house. In other words, they have the same mindset most young folks have in any construction project ... "We've got time, so let's build now and decorate later." In mid-life, that's not an option.

> **"We've got time, so let's build now and decorate later." In mid-life, that's not an option.**

For anyone past the age of 40, budgeting and planning for our comfortable enjoyment is what should matter most. And *comfort* translates into very basic decorating products and embellishments that all add up to big bucks when the bill comes in. No, it's not just new lamps and accessories but *real basics* for the kitchen and bath – and new bath towels and color coordinated everyday dishes are just the tip of the iceberg. No, not just new "pretty" towels, but actually replacing each and every towel throughout the house so that they're fresh and match the new surroundings.

And don't forget those other cost-adding touches like rematting the existing prints and artwork to go with the new house color scheme. New bed linens, cookware, floral arrangements – it's *all* of these little things that make a new house worth the effort and dollars spent on

> It's those little things that really make us feel good and comfortable within our house.

the actual construction. Unfortunately, those are the dollars most folks leave out or begrudgingly spend because they consider those items to be frivolous extras. If only they knew how important those *little extras* are in creating a comfortable home.

*N*ow for a dose of reality ... you *will* spend big bucks when you go to purchase all of these so-called "extras". Just think back to the last time you went to the local discount store to buy new dish towels and came through the check-out line $50.00 lighter. A few dish towels have a way of growing to include placemats, maybe some napkins and a new tablecloth. We just can't help it! It's those *little* things that really make us feel good and comfortable within our house, and unfortunately, even those little things add up to big bucks when you are buying to outfit a new home.

> **Go through every item ... from book to ashtrays to throw pillows ... put a replacement tag by each item in today's dollars, [and] add the cost of replacing [them]...now add a minimum of 25%...**

Wondering how much all of this new stuff will cost? As a professional who's seen every style and budget range for the past twenty years, I can truly say that it will cost a lot more than you think!

Want to prove me wrong? Take this little test. Go through *every* item, and I mean everything, from books to ashtrays to throw pillows, currently in your existing den. Put a replacement price tag by each item in today's dollars, add the cost of replacing your existing furniture and window treatments (don't just guess, actually visit a furniture store to really see the price tags), and don't forget area rugs, knick-knacks, lamps, light bulbs, stereo equipment, etc. Now add a minimum of 25% to the total price and then pick yourself up off of the floor.

See? It really adds up! And that's a total *before* you even add in the additional furniture it will take to fill up all of the extra square footage you're adding in the remodeling project or new house!

*B*y now you're probably thinking, "OK, I get it; I'll budget for the small stuff and come out ahead because I'll be keeping most of my furniture." *Wait* a minute! Stop and *think!* If the house you're building/remodeling is like most modern-day designs with high ceiling lines and wide-open floorplans, how is your existing furniture going to fit in? The furniture that was perfect 25 years ago in a little 12' x 15' living room with an 8 foot ceiling is not going to be of the correct scale and proportion, let alone style, for your new residence.

> **The furniture that was perfect 25 years ago is not going to be of the correct size and proportion, let alone style, for your new residence!**

By not actually planning and *budgeting* to purchase new pieces designed *specifically* for the new space, then all you have upon moving into your new house is a different place in which to clean your same old worn-out stuff!!

So what's the bottom line answer when you want to build a nice home, be comfortable and still have a few dollars left in the bank? It's simple if you follow this advice:

Only build what you can afford to decorate!

*W*ith that advice in mind, the way to approach any remodeling/building project is to:

• Start by assessing your real square footage needs and stop planning (and paying for) specialty areas such as a formal dining room especially if you only use it once a year! In other words, get realistic about your actual requirements. Cutting out the unimportant areas leaves more money to be spent on those spaces within our homes that matter most.

...get realistic about your actual requirements.

• *Discuss, plan and budget* with your partner the expected dollar amounts it will realistically take to complete the project in an all-inclusive "soup to nuts" fashion and *stick to it!* It's so very important to keep in mind the end result at all times. After all, if you're going to go through the hassle of building or remodeling, you need to keep a clear vision of

...keep a clear vision of that final end result of comfort.

the big picture and that final end result of *com-fort*. Why torture yourself if you're not going to be surrounded in a comfortable environment when the project is finished?

DESIGN BASICS ...

Repairing the walls in bathrooms where the wallpaper has peeled and the paint has chipped is easy to fix if you start at the beginning. Strip off all existing paper, and lightly sand the walls after filling any holes or feathering ripped sheet rock with a thin coat of spackling compound. Next paint the walls with one coat of cheap latex flat and then coat the walls with a quality "size" agent. Now hang solid vinyl paper instead of standard wallpaper ... the extra care spent on the prep work and by using the correct wallcovering product will ensure a care-free bath for years to come!

Tired of the "grasscloth wallpaper below the chair rail" look? No wonder, it's been around for almost 20 years! Start to change this dated style by just springing for a can of paint. That's right, you can actually paint the grasscloth and other natural wallcoverings with any good quality latex satin paint. Since the surface of the old grasscloth will be really dry and brittle, be prepared to apply at least 3 coats for full coverage.

A good contractor-grade tape measure is considered one of the most basic of tools – so why do I continually see folks struggling to use them? Could be that no one ever taught us how to use this tool properly. Here's how it works: just use your index finger under the tape as you pull it from the metal case. Apply pressure along the underside of the metal tape anywhere that you want to stop the tape; the pressure from your finger will stop the tape from retracting back into the case.

See? That was easy!

Got a laminate kitchen or bath countertop that needs a quick face lift? Try a little furniture polish! That's right, enhance the luster by spraying quality furniture polish directly onto the countertop, letting the whitish spray sit for about 2 minutes and then wiping it off in a circular motion with a clean cotton cloth. You'll just love the fresh appearance of your old countertop!

For a total designer looking bath, don't forget the small details. Be sure to update and replace worn and ugly towels, mildewed shower curtains, and ratty looking bath mats. Usually one year of everyday use will render these items a helpless case of the "uglies". So remember, even the most handsome and well designed of rooms still needs attention to the small details of everyday living long after the project is completed.

When building a new home or attempting a major remodel of your present house, don't forget the number-one rule of design...only build what you can afford to decorate! Nothing is worse than having a brand new house with nothing in it but your same old worn out stuff! Remember, sometimes smaller square footage is better if it means that you can comfortably enjoy/afford all of your efforts in a completed decorative style!

To make any black wrought iron piece look like the new **VERTIGRIS FINISH** (swirly marble look) this tip is quick and easy, but extremely messy - so be sure to cover the floor with a good drop cloth.

Start by cleaning the metal with **0000** steel wool to remove any rust or light dirt. Next, rip a small section of a household sponge (cutting with scissors will not give the same effect) and dip lightly into oil base paint. I recommend Sherwin Williams #1203 alkyd gloss, but any dark blue-green teal color will work. Apply the paint-dipped sponge in a blotchy pattern over the entire piece making sure to leave several sections of the original black color showing through.

Before the paint starts to dry and become dull begin this next step. Using a small cheap nylon paint brush, break the bristles by crushing the tips into the palm of your hand to create a perfect "effects" tool. With a light twisting motion, twirl the dry brush through the still-wet paint. This will automatically drag and swirl the paint into the light and feathery pattern found in expensive **VERTIGRIS FINISH** furniture.

After the swirled paint has dried completely, you can add a protective finish to your
"new piece".

Update your den by painting the paneling.
Here's how: start by washing the paneling with
a vegetable-based soap to remove cooking
grease and furniture polish. Next, lightly sand
the wood using 0000 sand paper (extra fine)
by sanding in the direction of the grain. Wipe
off the dusty film before you apply an alkyd
primer. To save you time, this primer can be
tinted to 75% strength of the final top coat
color. If there has been excessive cigarette
smoke or heavy cooking grease left to build up
on the walls, you'll need a shellac-based
primer. Keep in mind that all primers are different than regular paint and require separate
clean-up tricks, so ask the paint store clerk to
assist you on selecting the right one for your
job.

After the primer has dried for at least 24
hours, you're ready for the last step. The
TYPE of paint you select for the top coat will
be based on how you intend to use the room.

For homes with sticky little fingers or cleaning concerns, use an alkyd semi-gloss, otherwise, latex enamel or even latex flat paint will do.

Hate the look of the sprayed popcorn ceilings found in most smaller homes? Here's how to paint it: using a light colored latex flat paint and a small angled trim brush, paint a 6 inch wide band around the ceiling line, close to the walls. Since the texture is so hard to completely cover, a darker color will allow the white background to be visible against the contrast, so be sure the color you select is within a pastel range. Next, using a high nap roller cover, simply roll the ceiling like you would paint the walls. The only difference is that you want to make sure you keep plenty of paint on the roller, and never dry out the roller between trips to the paint pan (this will loosen the sprayed sheetrock particles causing them to fall). Before painting a light second coat, be sure to wait 24 hours in order to let the paint AND the underneath sheetrock mud particles dry.

For decorative exterior accents near the front door, terra cotta planters are a great idea if they are sized correctly. I recommend using a minimum size of 20 inches. This seemingly oversized pot will be in perfect balance with the overall size of the door and the exterior facade of the house. Now for the hard part – to get the correct size balance of the planted pot, be sure to add a few bricks to the bottom of the pot prior to adding a 4' tall shrub or tree. This will ensure the correct drainage and also adjust for the height.

The trick here is to keep the shrub in the original black plastic container before you add it to the decorative pot. I found that common dogwoods, Alberta spruce and Japanese maples will do well in most parts of the country and will remain in the original nursery container for several years with just minimal care.

Simply place the bricks in the bottom of the terra cotta pot. Then lower the black container shrub into the terra cotta pot so that it is resting on top of the bricks. This will raise the rim of the black plastic container so that it is almost level with that of the terra cotta pot.

Now all you have to do is fill with mulch the empty space between the black container and the terra cotta pot. WOW! Now it looks like you've planted the shrub directly into the terra cotta.

If birds are your passion, don't forget to consider your home's exterior architectural styling whenever selecting bird houses and feeders. Complement your exterior color scheme by arranging feeders so that overly bright containers will be away from the sight line of the body of the house. And to help hide the scattered seed mess, plus add a nice land-scaping touch to the base of the feeders, add a few sun ferns around the base (the variety KIMBERLY QUEEN seems to do well in most climates).

Position deck and patio furniture for con-versation and comfortable relaxation. Just like in your living room, be sure to position a small table or natural ledge close to every seating group. This is ideal for resting a snack tray or holding a tall cool beverage. A serving cart is also a great investment in entertaining as well as a functional piece of decoration. The two shelf variety may cost a few dollars more, but it also can serve as a plant stand to display all of your shade-loving annuals and plants.

Remember you are decorating outside so be sure to include LOTS of outdoor ambiance such as potted plants, over-scale potted shrubs and even potted trees associated with decks and patios. Don't forget to arrange the plants much like your interior accessories by grouping together 3 terra cotta pots (18", 20" & 24" in diameter) filled with dark green **NELLI STEVENS** holly shrubs and a 6' dogwood tree. WOW! What an impressive decorative accent for that empty shady corner on the deck! And to finish the look, I always like to add to the shrub by tucking a large pot of green ivy around the rim of the terra cotta so that the ivy cascades down the front.

Spruce-up an old concrete birdbath by giving it a bath of color. Simply take a blue-green oil based paint (Sherwin Williams #2257 works the best) and thin it 75% with mineral spirits. Then brush the mixture onto the concrete surface. Once the paint dries and has fully soaked into the concrete, simply smear the entire birdbath with vanilla yogurt. (Who said I can't cook?!!) Now it will be ready for the final touch - a good long burial! That's right, just dig a hole and bury the birdbath for about two months. When you dig it up, the yogurt will have aged to a mossy green color and the thinned paint will be a perfect accent color for the newly "ANTIQUE" birdbath.

Arranging outdoor patio and deck furniture for an attractive comfortable look can be tricky unless you consider the overall height of the house, existing tree line, and of course, the sky. To make it simple, imagine the outside perimeter of the deck as if it had 20' tall walls. Next imagine an oversized area rug in the center of the deck. Allowing for ample walkways, now arrange the furniture in the location of this imaginary rug so that from each chair and chaise one can converse EASILY without having to raise your voice over a normal speaking level. Now step back and look at your furniture grouping as it appears in front of the nearby

landscaping and against the imagined 20'
walls. This gets a little tricky, but really try to
imagine the scene behind the furniture as if it
were a framed landscape hanging on those 20'
high walls.

Once you've "seen" the view and furniture
together you can now adjust the position of
each piece so that it complements the scenery
while still retaining function. Next you can add
the decorative "pretties" much the same as if
you were adding floor plants or lamps to your
living room furniture groupings.

The whole idea is to get you to think of decorating your outdoors as if it was an interior
room, only with really tall ceilings!

We add potpourri in our homes to lighten
our senses as well as please the eye, so be
sure to do the same in your outdoor gathering
areas. Plant fragrant jasmine and other sweet
smelling vines and plants nearby so that their
wonderful aroma wafts throughout the night
air as you entertain or simply relax with the
family after a hard day. Also consider burning
a few large incense cones in addition to the
typical citronella candles. I like the natural

vanilla musk. It mixes well and covers up the bug smell without defeating the purpose.

For exterior decoration, nothing looks more attractive than shutters, but only if they are on the appropriate style of house. A traditional brick or simple frame style house looks the best when dressed out with shutters. A frame house with extremely high pitch rooflines and contemporary-style long windows does not show design savvy if you use more traditional or colonial styled shutters.

Instead, check out canvas awnings for decorative accent on contemporary-styled homes. The new materials, colors and super strong framework make awnings the perfect choice for curb appeal.

Play up your home's exterior with curb appeal. To get a few ideas, drive through a few neighborhoods and take notes on those homes that catch your attention. You'll soon notice that all of these houses create something special near the front door. Depending on the architectural style, this could be decorative wide moldings that surround the door, an attractive canvas awning covering the front entry, beautiful potted shrubbery at either side of the entry, or something as simple as a shiny brass knocker and kick plate.

You'll also notice recessed lighting instead of side surface-mounted light fixtures. The light cast from the ceiling fixtures will illuminate the entire front entry and make the space inviting and attractive. With light only coming from side-mount fixtures, the only thing you're going to see at night is the bright light from the fixture itself as it glares and obscures your home's beauty.

Some of my thoughts on decorating are totally unique & different from the other design gurus – stick with me – I promise you'll learn something new every page.

*N*ow that I've got you thinking about *comfort* as the final goal in any remodeling and building project, why not take the time to jot down your comfort requirements *before* starting your next project ... You'll be amazed at the way you now see the project when you look at it and plan for it with *comfort* in mind.

Design Notes ...

_____

_____

_____

_____

_____

_____

_____

_____

_____

_____

**Only build what you can
afford to decorate.**

chapter four

THE EYES HAVE IT
Observe, Create, Decorate

 $\mathcal{I}$ 've always considered the initial client - designer interview to be a vital part of the design process. It's that first phase of every project where I start to develop a plan which will eventually lead to a warm and comfortable home. During this meeting, I usually gather the information necessary to understand the overall project and get specific data about the actual remodeling / construction portion. While there are many factors to consider (budget, time frame, style, construction elements, weather, etc.), this section of our meeting generates results and usually goes by quickly. However, when the discussion turns to personal preferences, expectations for the final project, and comfort levels, it sometimes seems to take forever!

As a professional, I've been trained to seek answers to those personal factors prior to making my recommendations. Otherwise, I'm doing the client a disservice, wasting my time and their money if I don't understand exactly what it is that they like. So why is it so hard for folks to express their preferences, expectations and comfort levels? Well, the answer is simple -- they don't know what they like. Most of them only know what they *don't* like. Having to verbally describe what they expect "comfort" and "warm and friendly" to look like is impossible.

> **Having to verbally describe what "comfort" and "warm and friendly" look like is impossible.**

But in the end, they all tell me *exactly* what it is that they want – except they're not using words to communicate. I've found that most of the answers to my questions concerning preferences and comfort levels can be garnered if I just *open my eyes, listen with my heart* and *read between the lines.*

*B*ecause of my hectic travel schedule, I get to see small towns and the surrounding outskirts of large cities as I pass to and from my business destinations. Driving through these areas, I can't help but wonder what it would be like to live there. But the only way that I have to evaluate these areas are from subtle clues that I can immediately see as I drive by. In other words, it's my first impression that will form my opinion of that town and the people who live there.

> **"Dear God! The very houses seem asleep; and all that mighty heart is lying still."**
> **– Wordsworth, 1807**

Just like your Mom always told you, "It's those little nice things that count." So it is because it *is* those things that shape my passerby opinion. If a small town has strip mall parking lots filled with trees and shrubbery throughout the streetscape and large trash and recycling containers nicely concealed, I immediately get the impression that the townspeople care about their home place, and are united together in the same social status to be able to enforce zoning and other requirements to maintain an attractive town. What I see tells me that the townspeople care.

If, however, I see tractor-trailer storage units parked on the main street, abandoned and/or neglected store-fronts, and sidewalks missing or in need of long overdue repair, the picture I imagine about the town's resi-

> **We don't always have the time to devote to a lengthy examination before we arrive at an impression.**

dents is one of social inequity, apathy for group and individual welfare, and a total disregard for the neighborhood. I also drive by with the feeling that this is not a true community, but a place where the residents merely exist.

Sure, I can find pockets of attractive neighborhoods and areas where a glimpse of community exists, but over-all, the town is not functioning as a unit. A town like this would not be my first choice to live in. I know this judg-ment may seem quick and harsh, but that's life! In the times we live in, unfortunately we don't always have the time to devote to a lengthy examination before we arrive at an impression. And the only way I have to evaluate a town as I drive by at 50 miles an hour is through the use of my eyes and my own personal evaluation for comfort. Too bad I'll miss getting to know a few good people living in those run-down towns; but again ... that's life and we all miss out.

Now before you think of me as snobbish, just think back to *your* last vacation when you walked into that unfamiliar hotel lobby. You immediately formed an impression about the room awaiting you just by the condition and the scent of the lobby. Or what about the seafood restaurant that had a great location, but the condition of

...impressions of the surroundings do play a large part in your evaluation of the place and the people who live / work there.

the dining area and the stained and dirty appearance of the serving staff had you wondering about the quality – let alone sanitary conditions – of the food served? See, impressions of the surroundings *do* play a large part in your evaluation of the place and the people who live or work there.

Face it … We make appearance judgements *all day long*. And these opinion-forming impressions to your surroundings and environment are most noticeably present only during your first visit or initial encounter with a new location. After you've become accustomed to the situation, place, restaurant, town, whatever, your "evaluation antennae" – that part of your being that lets you clearly *see* and *read* between the lines – takes a back seat to complacency.

> **"The real problem in life is to have sufficient time to think."**
> **– Sir Edward Heath**

Haven't you ever heard of the old saying, "You're too close to the situation and can't see it clearly?" Well, the same is true when it comes to evaluating and redecorating your own home, business or even a town – sometimes you're just too close to the situation to really *see* it. Because you've become complacent and adjusted to the surroundings, your intuitive evaluation antennae are just not working. Most homeowners aren't even aware of the condition of their own "home-style" and what it's saying about them to any visitor or acquaintance. And those that know they need a spruce-up have difficulty doing so because they just can't *see* clearly what needs fixing. Therefore, they just can't seem to make any headway in their quest for comfort.

It's no wonder that most people want to redecorate for comfort, but have trouble achieving that end result because *they are blind to what they have to work with*. In other words, they are too close to the situation to get the clarity needed for that all-important first decorating impression. They just can't *see* the obvious.

> ...sometimes you're just too close to the situation to really see it.

For the town resident, it may be an old and peeling billboard that tells visitors that this is not a place where people care. And the business owner has a hard time *seeing* that his reception room decorating style (featuring uncomfortable orange chairs from the '70s) is sending out *big* signals that his company is offering old and outdated merchandise. Then there's the average homeowner who spends big dollars on new window treatments in hopes of giving the living room an inviting look when all it needed was to get rid of the clutter. If only they all could see with fresh "evaluation antennae" which allow open eyes to see and read between the lines of decorating know-how.

*S*o how do you get that ability to see with first-time impression clarity when it's your everyday home? How can you step back far enough to really see as if you were a first time visitor? Easy – open your eyes and really look! After all, before you can create and decorate you have to be able to observe the situation clearly in order to achieve the desired results.

What is the first step in *opening eyes* so that awareness, change, remodel, and redecoration can begin? The answer is simple. Take a photo! Just by looking at a photo of a space we've personally seen thousands of times we can begin to

> ...before you can create and decorate you have to be able to observe the situation clearly in order to achieve the desired results.

open our eyes to *really* see. You'll be amazed at what shows up in the photo that you never even noticed. Those "little" things that are missing or need adjusting that you just *didn't see* because you were too busy living there: the undersized furniture as compared to the size of the fireplace, or the kids' toys and school books stashed on the bookcase among the pile of VCR tapes and empty CD cases – and the list goes on.

Through the use of a photo, we can step *away* from our everyday complacency and existing decorating style and are now able to assess the situation through the eyes of a first-time observer. Only then can we make a *true* and almost unbiased evaluation, which is necessary before any change can occur. The bottom line simple advice is this: if you want to redecorate your home for comfort, take a photo to *really see* what needs changing!

> **If you want to redecorate your home for comfort, take a photo to really see what needs changing!**

The next step is to evaluate the space and *observe* what is currently *not* comfortable and *listen* to that little voice that gives you *first impression clarity* immediately upon viewing the photo of your space. And lastly, *read* between the lines of this chapter. Before you can add or change for comfort, you first have to *see*.

*B*efore you can *observe*, *create*, or *decorate* you first have to open your eyes and turn on your "evaluation antennae". Do that by taking lots of photographs of the rooms to be redecorated, remodeled or spruced-up. You'll be surprised at what you really *see*! Do yourself a big favor and start *every* project by becoming *aware* through the use of photos. Then, when you think you're finished with the project, take another photo just to see if you haven't missed an opportunity for a few final touches that only *fresh eyes* can see. Believe me ... the results will be well worth the extra effort and few dollars the film will cost. Be on the lookout for these "comfort busters" while observing your before-and-after photos:

- Straggly and dying plants

- Deflated and worn-looking throw pillows

- Small rips and dangling threads on upholstered furniture in addition to sagging cushions and worn areas

- Wall paint colors that are too light or too dark a background choice for your furniture color

- Draperies that are too short and drooping at the rod

- Patches of dark, dismal areas instead of an even flood of light throughout the entire room.

- Furniture wedged tightly up against the walls instead of more comfortably positioned towards the center of the room. Even in small rooms, be sure to leave at least 6" between the wall and back of sofas and upholstered chairs, etc.

- Accent and club chairs too far apart from the main seating group. While seated, if you have to raise your voice above a normal speaking tone, you're too far apart.

Now that you know how to have "fresh eyes" –
go back and re-read chapters 1-3 –
I guarantee you'll learn more the
second time around.

DESIGN BASICS ...

Considering a new paint color for that dark bedroom? Well, don't select the lightest shade on the chart unless you want the room to look gray and washed out! For any space that is lacking in natural light, always select a paint color that is in the middle of the charts. Once it is on the walls, it will actually appear lighter and seem to make the room more inviting. If you selected the lightest color, once on the walls, it will only look "blah" – leaving you with a freshly painted but dark and dreary bedroom.

Take a photo of your kitchen to see what it looks like to a visitor and then work on cleaning away any cluttered areas. Sorry, but empty vitamin bottles, dying plants, and last year's calendars are decorating nightmares!

Test-drive your guestroom! Yep, that's right. Go ahead and spend the night, complete with packed luggage, in the room where you expect your overnight or weekend guests to say during their visit to your home. Be sure to check out the room for basics: towels, bed

linens, a place to unpack and arrange toi-
letries, and privacy (both sound an physical). A
lot of folks tend to forget about the most basic
of human needs that calls for some privacy. If
your guestroom doesn't prevent the occupant
from directly knowing the private business of
others in the house be sure to install a radio
or TV in the guestroom. It's these little things
that will help make your guestroom extremely
attractive and comfortable to both guest and
family members alike.

Tired of ready-made bed linens always looking skimpy? Next time buy bed comforters and
dust ruffles one size larger than the bed it's
intended for. The cut of the next larger size
will make up for the skimpy fullness factor
found in most ready-made products. Don't
worry, the larger comforter will look luxurious,
but to hide the white platform section of the
oversized skirt, you'll need to gather up the
excess in a straight line and pin it to the top of
the box spring. See ... a simple way to go from
skimpy to luxury!

Can't afford new den furniture? How about rethinking the furniture arrangement so that you eliminate the sofa and loveseat and use multi-function club chairs instead. They are much more reasonably priced than a sofa, and with a little luck, you can even get a great deal on used club chairs which can be recovered to coordinate with your color scheme.

Simply arrange the individual chairs as you would the sofa and loveseat and be sure to put a nifty sofa table behind one of the chair groupings. This will help to pull the look together. HINT: If you buy new or just recover the chairs, you'll most likely receive fabric arm covers. Do not use these arm covers. New advances in fabric construction make the underside of the fabric just as durable and tough as the topside. If an arm cover is placed over the top of an upholstered arm it will wear and abrade the fabric underneath. Keep the arm covers around only for fabric repair in case of jagged tears and burn holes.

To keep your house fresh-smelling, hand fluff and lightly crush loose potpourri daily making sure to keep it in a wide-mouth container instead of a small jar or vase. All of the fragrant petals, pods and fillers need continual movement in order to circulate the great aroma beyond the bowl and into your rooms.

Got an oil painting that's looking old and dusty? If it's not an investment piece, clean the canvas by spraying a good grade of furniture polish directly on the painting and rubbing in a circular motion with a clean white cotton cloth. The wax will help loosen any dirt and also protect the glossy finish of the canvas.

Can't seem to get your glass doors, windows, mirrors, and artwork glass really clean and free from streaks? Well, ditch the paper towels and pick up yesterday's newspaper. The stiffness and absorbent qualities of wadded newsprint will actually clean and polish the glass instead of just wiping up the cleaning solution!

Want a simple no-sew decorative treatment for a small boring bedroom window? Just remove the existing curtain and leave the basic white rod installed. Using one rectangular bed pillow sham, remove the pillow insert and then drape the empty sham over the rod so that it forms a triangle. Allow the point of the triangle to hang down about 15 inches. Instant style for a special bedroom!

Ever wonder why the magazine homes all seem to have really luxurious-looking drapery treatments even if the style is just a simple throw style? Well, the answer lies in the lining. To make sure the draperies hang with a softer and more expensive looking fold, an additional fabric layer known as **INNERLINING** is used between the face and lining fabrics. It's a fibrous plain fabric, much like flannel. It helps to soften while giving extra depth to the body of the chintz drapery panels. And it's this inexpensive (about $4 per yard) innerlining that makes the window treatment look so rich and sumptuous.

Using hardback books on small chair-side tables is a great way to add a nice comfortable touch to any room. Start by grouping the books according to size, color, and shape; subject matter doesn't count here. All you're interested in is the color of the spines of the books. Next place a few coffee table-sized books under a lamp positioned towards the back of the chair-side table. This will help make the lamp more attractive and seem more expensive. Or you could just stack three art books on a chair-side table and display family photos on top ... instant decorating that says COMFORT! And, if your house has a contemporary setting, try this idea as a chair-side table: a 20 inch terra cotta planter with a 30 inch piece of 1/2 inch thick beveled glass over the top. This would look great beside a sunroom chair.

Have your ceiling fans started to show their age? Well, LOOK UP and really LOOK! I can assure you that every new visitor to your home has noticed the inch thick layer of dust on that old out-of-date wicker blade. So if you can't replace the fans, how about a good cleaning and then painting to bring them up to date?

It's easy, here's how: Safety first - start by flipping the breaker that controls the fan to the **OFF** position. Next remove the blades or paddles taking extra care not to remove any brass or decorative metal which appears to have been molded rather then screwed onto the unit. Clean the blades with a mild soap and damp cloth. Then rinse with a vinegar and water solution. After this dries for at least 4 hours, sand and fill any scratches or nicks on the blade surfaces.

Using an oil-base or alkyd primer, apply the primer using wide and long brush strokes going in the direction of the blade. After 24 hours drying time you're finally ready to paint! A top-quality spray enamel paint will give the best finish so don't skimp on the price or the number of cans. A 5" blade fan usually takes 2 cans to cover completely.

Start by coating each blade with a light misting of the finish color. Continue to "mist" paint each blade with several layers of spray paint until the color looks rich and even. This type of painting takes lots of time and patience but the finished product looks **FACTORY-FRESH**.

When using your ceiling fan remember these tips for a comfortable and energy efficient home:

· in warm weather, set the **REVERSE SWITCH** to produce a downward flow of air. For the winter months, be sure the blades are set to direct the air flow upward; this helps recover the wasted heat trapped at the ceiling and gently recirculates it to the floor. If the fan is installed over a table, be sure the blades are set for an upward flow of air; downward air flow would tend to quickly cool the meal and scatter products.

· for rooms with 8' ceilings always use a **HUGGER** model versus a short stem; these tend to look flimsy and are subject to wobble.

Time to recover the sofa? Remember these tips for a great-looking project:

· set the skirt height accordingly for the type of floor surface on which the sofa will sit. Since the front legs of the sofa will usually sink into a deep carpet, be sure to shorten the skirt of any upholstered piece scheduled for overtop of carpeting. On hardwood, the skirt can be set with a normal 1/2" clearance.

· remind the upholstery shop to match all patterns and cushion seams so as to be in perfect alignment with the pattern on the body of the sofa and **ALWAYS** instruct the upholster to check the fabric for flaws and yardage **BEFORE** cutting into the goods. Fabric manufacturers will relinquish responsibility on damaged goods once the fabric is cut. In other words, even if there is a big hole in the fabric, once the upholsterer cuts into the goods you're stuck because he didn't find the flaw before placing the first cut.

· **BE PATIENT.** The average length of time it takes to have a sofa recovered is generally 4-6 weeks, so chill out and dream about relaxing on your "new" sofa.

Remember – ALWAYS train
yourself to look at a room
with "fresh eyes".

Design Notes ...

_____

_____

_____

_____

_____

_____

_____

_____

_____

_____

_____

_____

**Open your eyes, see with your heart,
and read between the lines.**

chapter five

THE BALANCING ACT
Getting the Right Mix Between Comfortable and Trendy

*S*everal years ago I experienced the "light bulb moment" of my professional career. You know what I mean; it's that small phrase, action, or occurrence that makes you stop and *think*. It's as if a light bulb was turned on in your head and suddenly everything fell into place with such clarity that going back to the old ways of doing, thinking or acting is just no longer an option.

That's exactly what happened the day that TV personality Debbie Alan and I went shopping for her living room furniture. After a long day of decisions, we had come to our last item – the host accent chair for the living room "conversation grouping". This is the seating location where the homeowner usually positions herself in order to facilitate conversation and service among the invited guests. Some people even like to call it the "cat-bird" seat because you can see everything from this location. Anyway, we had tentatively selected a generously-sized English wing chair. The color and fabric pattern was perfect as shown. So with only the addition of a complementary down-filled accent pillow for the back of the chair, our work for the day was complete.

Design-wise, everything was wonderful – the chair was ideally scaled to complement the other furnishings and overall room size, the color and fabric worked together to form a beautiful balance within the overall house color palette, and the price was right! As the project designer wearing the "decorator hat", what more could I ask or even plan for? Well, everything was wonderful

Always keep a professional eye towards a totally balanced comfortable end result.

until petite 5' tall Debbie sat down in the chair. She had this strange little quirky look on her face and it took me a moment to recognize the cause. Even though the chair was perfectly balanced for all of the right design reasons, it did not fit *her* comfort level. As she sat there with her legs stuck out

> **"Getting your life and house in order are one and the same."**
> **– Deborah Burnett**

in front looking like Lily Tomlin's character "Edith Anne", I started to chuckle as that light bulb of understanding went off in my mind. Without balancing the comfort needs of people who will actually use the furniture, what good is the rest? I guess you could say, thanks to Debbie's short legs and wonderful personality, I now always keep a professional eye towards a *totally* balanced comfortable end result.

Just in case you're wondering how the room turned out ... in a word, *GREAT!* To solve the problem between design criteria and comfort needs, we accentuated the chair. We simply added two hard-filled down pillows to the back of the chair instead of one. This supported

Debbie's back while positioning her closer to the front of the seat cushion, which eliminated the "Edith Anne" look. And to balance out the over-pillowed chair, a wonderful knitted throw loosely draped across the chair arm did the trick. As a final touch to complete the comfort vs. "room design" imbalance, a small exposed-leg ottoman tucked beneath the chair served both the room's "look" and Debbie's personal comfort level quite well.

*N*ot long ago, I was enjoying a nice cup of coffee in a bookstore when the evening's entertainment commenced. A very attractive young musician had the attention of every female in the small store when he sat down to the microphone. But once the music started, everyone's thoughts had changed. Even though he was a very talented folksinger, the total presentation of his performance was irritating. You see, the amplifier on his guitar was turned up so high that you couldn't even hear his voice, let alone the melody, lyrics, or intent of his songs. It

> "Perhaps with age I've learned to let go of things and people, trying not to possess or confine them."
> – Tony Harrison

was such a shame – the beautiful evening, relaxing atmosphere, attractive performer, and the right mix – but wrong sound. The loud high-tech reverberations distorted the music so that we, the audience, only heard irritating noise.

For most, the experience of enjoying the total ambience of bookstore music is wonderfully relaxing. It's very similar to finding yourself adrift in deep contemplation while enjoying the performance of your church choir. No, I don't mean day-dreaming, but really listening and having your spirit filled with joy. Now just imagine the shock to your internal balance if, in the middle of this relaxing music, you suddenly hear over-amplified drums, horns and cymbals – all so loud you no longer hear the voices.

If this has never happened to you, then take this opportunity to go on a creative journey. Right now, close your eyes, put down the book, and imagine that you are quietly sitting and enjoying beautiful vocals from your favorite singer. You're really getting into the music and maybe even finding deep meaning to the lyrics

All of the instruments should blend together in background support of the vocals.

when all of a sudden the drums, piano, and other instruments are so over-amplified and gratingly loud that there is no way you can hear the voices let alone the lyrics! Now that's frustrating and also unfortunate because instrumental accompaniment is meant to *support* and not overpower the voices - all of the instruments should blend together in *background* support of the vocals.

So back to reality and the bookstore folksinger. That cute young man in the bookstore obviously didn't understand this basic tenet of enjoyable music – otherwise he would have "turned down" the irritating and distracting noise.

So, once again, what does all of this have to do with decorating? Well, just like instruments, it's that same background support of decorative accessories, color, texture and other details that all go into the performance of design. In other words, the final enjoyment of our decorating efforts all depends on the balance of the decorative "instruments" so as not to overpower the overall design "vocals". With a lack of concern for this basic tenet of design, only frustration can occur. A good example is that sense of frustration we get whenever we see a room decorating project that is almost "there" but not quite making it. And it's unfortunate, because usually a lot of money has been spent on select isolated individual items or areas

Background support and other details all go into the performance of design.

all without regard to the *background* support of the finished comfortable space. Again, too much "loud" support without regard to the overall room design.

I know this design basic of balance is hard to understand, so if you're having a difficult time following my instrumental support analogy as it relates to decorating, just read this next sentence out loud to better understand the thought and to have it really sink in - this is important.

When a lot of money has been spent on amplifiers (accessories, draperies, paint, etc.) without regard to the *overall* support of the vocals (function, comfort and enjoyment), the result is usually unfortunate and a decorating no-no.

With that thought in mind, think back to this scenario. Remember when you had first visited friends immediately after they've just finished that long dreamed about (and talked about) decorating project? Maybe they've just completed re-mod-

The skill of understanding and using balance is hard to come by.

eling, redecorating or building a new home ... or even if it was as simple as just upgrading a spare bedroom, they were proud of their finished work and invited you over to admire the results. You had to admit – it *did* look better than before, but something was still missing or out of place. It just didn't have that same feel as rooms you've seen illustrated in magazines or on TV. Maybe the room's paint color was okay but it's too bright a shade (think loud drums), or the window treatments are too "decorator looking" with all of those frills and accents (think too much emphasis in the soprano section), or the wallpaper is too busy (think over-zealous organ player) and the list goes on and on. Again, the background noise is *too* loud for the voices to be heard. The room design is overshadowed by the accessories, thus it's decorated but it just doesn't look like a room from a decorating magazine.

> **When a lot of money has been spent on amplifiers without regard to the overall support of the vocals the result is usually unfortunate.**

So why *is* there a difference between the magazine-finished rooms and your friends' house? Well, aside from a great lighting team, huge budget, and purposeful avoidance of room boo-boos, the magazine layout room has been thought out with a final balance in mind. You might think of it as *professionalism with an eye towards the finished project* – how it's going to be perceived, enjoyed and actually lived in. In a word, the room is totally planned for a complete balance of design and comfort. And, frankly, the skill of understanding and using *balance* is hard to come by. There are even a lot of decorators and some designers who have not yet mastered this art of the finished overall project, let alone understand the distinction, so give yourself some time to let this principle of design sink in.

Keep an eye towards the overall balanced finished project.

To compound matters, this very delicate and expensive art of decorating *balance* is now unconsciously expected of every homeowner thanks to countless magazine articles on decorating. The catch is this: layout photos are showing you the finished balanced room, so you can instantly recognize a space out of balance – but the magazines are not teaching you *how* to perform this decorating balance with an eye towards the finished project.

It's no wonder that you were able to notice that your friends' home was "nice but not quite there" but didn't exactly know why. So, to help you better understand the design basic of *balance* and to start your education in this most important aspect of design, check out the following homework assignments. They will give you a clue into the mindset of a professional on how to keep an eye towards the overall balanced finished project so that you too can listen to beautiful voices without the distraction of over-amplified instruments in *your* decorating projects.

$\mathcal{T}$o ensure that your next decorating project is totally balanced with an eye towards the finished *comfortable* end result, try out these tips:

• Take a photo of the project area room to better observe with "fresh eyes", making sure you assess the space with first time candor. Re-read chapter 4 to hone up on the technique.

• Spread out on the floor large swatches of the project's overall character - paint chips, all fabrics to be used in that space, samples of woods found in that room, and major accessory pieces, etc. Include anything that will have a bearing in conveying the room's finished "feel". Even if it's only a room "spruce up" and you'll be keeping your old furniture or stuck using your husband's old recliner, be sure to add a cushion or arm cover to the pile of swatches on the floor. In other words, if it's going to be *in, on* or *around* the project room, make sure you add a small sample of that object to the swatch pile.

• Arrange all of the swatches and representative samples in the order that they will be used. Do this by imagining a large rectangular shape in which you will be placing samples of the room to represent the actual location of the "real thing"... carpet swatch goes lower foreground, large paint sample middle area, with the fabric to represent the major upholstery pieces on top of the paint swatch. This will help you to "see" the sofa fabric as it will actually look when contrasted with the wall color.

If any one area / item stands out then you know it definitely will be out of balance once you complete the actual room.

• Once you've arranged all of the samples, swatches and items in the order that best represents the way they will used in the room, stand back at least 15 feet and really *look* at the collection. If any one area/item stands out like an overly-amplified folksinger then you know it *definitely* will be out of balance once you complete the actual room. Go back and modify your swatches, so that the "far away look test" is harmonious and pleasant. Don't make the mistake of trying to ignore a problem object or undesirable color that will be in the finished room – no matter how ugly or out of date, if you don't plan for that piece to be in the completed space, you'll *never* have a room with a professional eye towards the finished comfortable end result.

Balance is a hard concept
to understand; go easy on
yourself until you get it!

DESIGN BASICS ...

Whenever selecting a paint color from the store brand chips, keep in mind that the color will appear differently once on your walls ... in other words, most interior paint colors will appear lighter and brighter than what was represented on those tiny little paint chips. So anticipate the change, and buy the next "darker" shade of paint represented on the paint chart; on your walls, the dried paint will look like the chip sample you really liked!

Don't toss that cracked and split wooden salad bowl - it makes a great display piece for dried hydrangeas and other large floral stems. Start by spraying furniture polish directly on the wood and let the polish soak in. Next fill the bottom with potpourri and then gently heap a mound of pastel-tinted dried hydrangeas on top. Because the flowers are full and tend to overwhelm the bowl, one will never notice the crack or split condition of the wood.

Remember, in true design-savvy form, whenever there's a problem you can either camouflage it or accentuate the problem so that it looks like that's what you've intended to do all along - using the cracked salad bowl as a display base for fluffy flowers is actually doing both!

Want to make your bed so that it looks as comfy as those pictured in the magazines? If custom is out of your price range just buy a ready-made set one size larger than your bed size. The extra size and fabric lengths will look luxurious and better suited to today's over-sized scaled furniture sizes. Play up the colors by contrasting the sheet colors and be sure to add lots of throw pillows for a bed that's picture perfect!

Got a loveable house dog whose messy eating habits leave your nice clean floors all wet and messy? Circumvent the problem by raising the food and water dish; if a dog has to reach up and over to get to his food he's less likely to drip and spill all over your floor. So keep the dog (and your floor) happy by purchasing one of the new raised-dish pet serving stands. Several models are available for under $80 in most pet stores.

For extra clean glass surfaces, be sure to do like your granny always told you. First spray the cloth with a mild solution of vinegar and water, rub the glass vigorously in circles, let dry, then buff with a sheet of wadded up newspaper. The results will sparkle!

Chintz fabric is really a great choice whenever considering new draperies IF you know how to balance the stiffness of the fabric with the overall size of the window. A little confused? Well, first you have to understand the nature of chintz fabric - in a word, STIFF. The trick is to be able to balance this inherent stiffness with the "hang" appeal of today's soft and free flowing drapery styles. So the tip is simple; for a not-so-stiff chintz drapery window treatment, ADD more fabric!

Here's how: For a standard chintz side-panel drapery treatment I recommend using a 3 to 1 fullness ratio instead of the typical 2 to 1 fullness. If you sew, you'll know what I'm talking about. For those of you who don't know one end from the other of a sewing machine, just tell your drapery fabricator to increase the fullness to 3:1.

And for those of you working with store-bought panels, all you have to remember is this: for a 48 inch wide window, instead of buying one panel per side, plan on purchasing two panels per side. By beefing up the amount of fabric found in each side panel, the fabric will hang more tightly at the top and be forced to expand out from the mid-line down, giving the illusion of a softer "hand". (HAND: a drapery term that relates to the soft "hang appeal" of a fabric.) This will give your windows that custom look and appear totally different than those inexpensive ready-made chintz drapery panels which look skimpy and hang like stiff razor blades.

Most of the more expensive decorative fabrics have a wonderful hand in that they are soft, pliable, and drape or flow nicely much like they would when they are being used to decorate our homes. You can determine the "hand" of a fabric simply by rubbing the fabric between your own two hands and noticing how the fabric feels and drapes between your fingers and palms.

Stiff fabrics like chintz, linen, and some poplins all need special attention to fullness and lining selections in order to successfully use these fabrics for certain window treatments wherever a pliable hand is needed to achieve a soft and flowing style.

Whenever sprucing up your home, don't forget about the front door area. I like to consider this space as the "welcome mat to your personality." So why not play up this space with as much appeal as the rest of your home?

For traditional decor and architectural styling try this idea: using an oversized terra cotta container (I recommend the 24" diameter for best results), drop three bricks in the bottom of the pot so as to raise the interior bottom level by a few inches. On top of this, position a tall 5-7 gallon Alberta spruce or similar evergreen shrub. This variety is pretty hardy in most zones of the country, and with a little care, will do great for many years without need for transplantation. To the base of this shrub add a pot of glossy ivy so that it trails down over the lip and the side of the terra cotta pot.

For those of you who have a need for symmetrical balance, be sure to add two pots - one on each side of the door. In most cases, the proportion between the plants, pots and front door is perfectly balanced and will set the tone for a warm welcome into your comfortable home.

When arranging furniture in a small room it's best to use a little geometry! That's right - the old triangle theory of design. If you arrange the sofa so that it's caddy-corner in the center of the room, it usually makes the entire space seem more open and free-flowing.

The triangle comes into play when you position the TV directly in front of the sofa and add one chair to the wall side of the room. The best positioning is when this chair arm is actually within a few inches from the arm of the sofa. This angled arrangement allows for plenty of comfortable stretch-out room and makes conversation easy and enjoyable. Because of the close proximity of the seating, your family and guests will immediately feel a part of every conversation and activity.

This is in stark contrast to the typical living room arrangement of two chairs across from the sofa separated by a coffee table arrangement. This style of furniture arrangement is not only a dated relic from the '60s, but it also makes conversation stiff and almost impossible! Sometimes the distance between the seating is so great that each person has to shout to be understood.

Design Notes ...

_____

_____

_____

_____

_____

_____

_____

_____

_____

_____

_____

_____

_____

_____

_____

_____

_____

_____

_____

_____

_____

_____

_____

_____

_____

_____

_____

_____

_____

Study hard and practice often –
the skill of using balance correctly
is hard to come by.

chapter six

IN YOUR DREAMS
Learning to Tap into Your Creativity

*C*reativity ... that elusive trait so necessary for any new project to spring to life with a *sparkle* that rivals the brightest diamond. It's that special something that's hard to define but instantly recognizable whenever viewing an especially impressive design or decorating project. It's those rooms and spaces that seem to come alive with well-balanced color, interesting textures, a scale that perfectly suits the furnishings and a room that just feels so good you want to stay. Everything about it spells *comfort* with an uncommon creative edge. Wouldn't it be great if everyone could create that special something in their everyday design and decorating projects? I say, "Why not?" What's keeping *you* from creating your especially impressive home? Could it be that you've never been taught how to be creative?

Over these past 20+ years of my professional design and construction practice, I've had to fine-tune my creative skill in order to call it up at a moment's notice. During my many opportunities to "create" I've noticed a reoccurring method that never fails in allowing me to tap into my creative talents. With a little understanding and concentrated effort, you too can tap into *your* creative abilities.

$\mathcal{W}$henever I am speaking or presenting a semi-nar at conventions, women's groups, or even to a class of other designers, the folks coming up afterwards all seem to be interested in the same thing. "Where do you get your inspiration?" and "How do you come up with the ideas you show on TV?" They *really* want to know how I'm able to seemingly create something out of nothing or, as my sister-in-law phrased it, create a silk purse out of a sow's ear.

I tell them the answer is two-fold. All you have to do is understand that: (1) the answer is simple and available to everyone; and (2) to get to the simple answer you first have to rethink the way you approach decorating, design and life.

Let's start with # 1 first – the simple answer part. I'm creative and continue to get my imaginative ideas because God designed me that way. As such, I've always

> **"God has blessed me with the ability to see things "finished" – if only you could see what's in my head!"**
> **– Deborah Burnett**

known that I've had creativity and been blessed with what I like to call "the ability to see things finished." By this I mean that whatever I imagine, dream-up or plan for, I have been able to close my eyes and, all of a sudden, "see" the finished project as clear as if it were a photograph.

From the time I was a little girl building Barbie doll-houses out of shoe boxes and old glass jars, I have been able to mentally paint the projected decorating picture with such finite detail that its clarity would rival reality.

Now for the simplistic answer of #1; I truly believe that all of mankind already has the ability to actually visualize clear and finished results from their dreams and plans. Everyone has the ability to see things finished. We all can do this with such clarity, that *all* details are visible – unfortunately, most folks are just not using it!

> "Do what you can, with what you have, where you are."
> – Theodore Roosevelt

Now for the hard part, the second portion of the two-fold answer to the question, "How and where do you get your ideas and inspiration?" I can honestly say that my design creativity is based on the fact that *nothing* is new in design – it's just presented in a new light. I just happen to always be looking for and finding new ways to *present* design instead of wasting my time on discovering *new* design. Once you understand the basic principles of balance, light, proportion, scale, color, texture, budget, and comfort, everything in good design is the same; so in essence, *nothing* is new in design except for the way it's presented.

> **Once you understand the basic principles, everything in good design is the same.**

Think about it – a well-designed table top grouping of a lamp, stack of books, plant, and photo frame is the same no matter if it's done using decorative items from the '40s or from today – it's only the *style* of those accessories that is different. I guess you could say that the reason why I'm able to appear unusually creative by making a collection of mismatched yard sale items look attractive and fashionable is my understanding of the never-changing aspects of balance, light, proportion, scale, color, texture, budget, and comfort.

With these basic elements and principles in mind, it's easy for anyone to get creative whether arranging junk on a table top, or working with expensive and fashionable accessories – it doesn't make any difference because, if it's arranged correctly, anything can be well-designed!

*S*ince understanding and utilizing the gift of creativity can be difficult to tap, here's a little trick that I've found to be helpful. Whenever I want to "see things finished" I just pretend that I'm a movie set director. In other words, whenever I'm in the preliminary planning stages of a room design, I simply close my eyes and imagine myself walking onto a movie set.

Of course the set is *exactly* like the room I'm working on. As the set director, I'm walking through my imaginary room with a critical eye, always keeping in mind the camera's viewpoint. I first check out the room layout and overall color scheme so that no one color is really "hot" and jarring against the other colors found on the set. Next, I mentally position the camera in the doorway and check out the room

> **There is nothing new in design except for the way it's presented and perceived.**

from that angle looking for any obstructions the camera might see. I continue to do this around the entire room, all the while checking for the major design principles of balance, color, texture, comfort, function, scale, and proportion. (I already have the budget aspect covered.)

Once I'm satisfied that my plan will balance on my mental movie set, I then step back as set director and walk onto the set as the client who will actually live in the finished room. I walk around the room and use the space much like the client will eventually occupy that room. If it's a teenager's bedroom, I nap and lounge on the bed seeking comfort and telephone chat space. If the room I'm designing is a kitchen for a busy family, I pretend that I'm the mom trying to get dinner ready on a

> **In the preliminary planning stages of a room design, simply close your eyes and imagine yourself walking onto a movie set.**

night that schedules are a nightmare and everyone's running late. In other words, this section of my movie is devoted to checking out the usability and comfort levels of the room. Hey – don't forget – all of this is still in my head! The entire "movie set" is nothing more than a refined visualization of my preliminary plan for whichever space I'm designing/decorating. So if the kitchen in my head-movie won't work it certainly won't be usable in real life.

By now you're thinking either "She's a real fruit-loop," or "Great idea, but I'll never be able to do it!" Well, the amazing part of this technique is that with just a little practice and overcoming the fear of "someone's going to think me weird," *anyone* can do this. Remember back to the start of this chapter when I said that in response to the question of how I get my ideas that the answer was simple? Here it is again. Don't forget that *anyone* can create this imaginary movie and see the finished results because God designed us *all* with the ability to do so *if* we just let it happen. So come on – *let it happen*. You're not going to be successful at creativity until you realize you already have that ability and can be successful at it. And as for personal success at cre-

> You're not going to be successful at creativity until you realize you already have that ability and can be successful at it.

ative decorating/design, all you have to do is *always* keep in mind the basic elements and principles of design:

> Balance
>
> Proportion
>
> Light
>
> Color
>
> Scale
>
> Texture
>
> Budget
>
> Function
>
> Comfort

*T*o further help you on the quest for tapping into your own creativity, check out how I prepare for each and every one of my TV appearances.   You'll see that the movie set idea comes in handy not only for real-life projects but for creating TV design segments as well.

On a typical TV design segment for HGTV, TNN, QVC or any of the major networks, the prep work is always the same. After the producer and I collaborate on the topic and the slant to take while presenting that topic, my next step is to take a break and allow time to "just think". My mind is wandering and relaxing and suddenly the seed of an idea comes through. I then contemplate variables, challenges and other potential pitfalls about the proposed segment. Once these real-life hurdles are cleared, I set about planning my segment

> **"For different results, do something different!"**
> **– Unknown**

using mini-movie visualization – a "quickie" version of my full-scale movie technique, only this time, applying the basics of design to each and every step.

When I am able to "see" the segment from a balanced viewpoint, I then begin to pull props, tools needed for demonstration clarity, examples of "before-and-afters" and anything else the segment calls for. Several days later, when all of the props and other items are collected and organized (PROPORTION & SCALE) in the way I visualized in my mini-movie, I'm now ready to go through the movie set in my mind. As imaginary set director, I'm checking out how the presentation will look from the perspective of the camera and audience. Will the colors of my props and wardrobe be appropriate for the segment? Will there be balance and contrast with the real-life TV studio set? (COLOR & LIGHT) Will the point that I'm demonstrating be visually interesting? (TEXTURE) In essence, I'm giving it a test run to see if the ideas will actually work (FUNCTION) on camera for both me and the audience.

Put on a big smile and prepare to go through with the project.

In my imaginary "quickie" for the proposed TV segment, I next imagine myself actually doing the segment. I actually speak out loud while "seeing" myself do the segment as if it were real – in essence, to get the feel (COMFORT) of the segment. But sometimes, the usual 6-8 minutes air-time allowed (BUDGET) is not enough time to complete the segment in the format I've imagined. So I simply adjust my plan and my movie takes a slightly different course, readjusting for the changes. Once done mentally, I now feel comfortable in knowing that I can actually perform the given segment in the time allowed once the real-life cameras start rolling!

When it comes time to prepare for the TV host questions that I will face, I imagine what I expect each host to say and mentally pose the questions that they would ask. Then, in my "movie", I do a run-through with me actually playing the parts of whichever host I'm appearing with that day. Most of the time it's easy to predict the outcome, but sometimes, on the network

Daydream about how you'd like the space to look and feel.

shows or especially on the TNN show CROOK & CHASE, the unpredictability of the real-life situation and the hosts' "hits from left field" make full preparation rather difficult

– but *always* fun! That's when I quit trying to mentally prepare, and just rely on my real life experience, professionalism and sense of humor to carry me through. (BALANCE) It may sound zany, but this pretend movie set technique has been a successful guideline in helping me to communicate my thoughts and ideas onto the small screen for more than a decade. And because of this visualization technique, with regard to design basic principles, the audience always understands and appreciates my creativity and knowledge.

So how is this TV prep story going to help you decorate your living room? Well, very easily, *if* you go back and re-read the first portion of this story. There you'll find the answer to developing your decorating creativity. By doing so, you'll also recognize the key ingredients of any successful trait or talent:

- Taking time to really think about the challenge or problem

- Daydreaming about the problem and how you are going to solve it

- Imagining yourself in the situation and handling all obstacles

- Actively preparing for the challenge ahead

- Enjoying the situation as it takes place

Now, let's add the specific decorating skills to this equation for success. Pretend you want to redecorate your living room. Try this: *Sit back and relax* on a quiet day and really look about the current living room. *Daydream* about how you'd like the space to look and feel. *Would it be comfortable?* Would the kids be too rough on the arrangement in your mind? If so, change it to suit – after all it's in your head and you can do anything! Go ahead and *prepare the budget* or estimate to actually carry out your project. If you can't afford to do it all at once, prepare your time frame and budget to allow for incremental decorating so that in the end, the project will turn out *just* like in your head. Now back in the real world, *put on a big smile* and prepare to go through with the project in the time frame and budget you've allowed, all the while keeping in mind that *there will be* challenges ahead – husbands who can't understand why the 15-year-old sofa has to be replaced, workmen who don't show up, and so on.

So, for the connection between my TV segment preparation and decorating? Now you know – it's all just a movie in your head!

DESIGN BASICS ...

Like the look of down-filled throw pillows but can't afford the high price tag? Simple. Just open the top seam of a ready-made pillow (about a 5 inch opening) and reach in to remove several handfuls of the filling. Once the outer fabric is slightly mushy just sew back the seam. Complete the look by cinching a tasseled drapery tie-back around the pillow.

Old lace tablecloths make great window treatments for a country casual home. Here's how: using a rectangular open-weave lace tablecloth, arrange the fabric in 6" accordion pleats. Determine the center and equally space the cloth over the top of a standard curtain rod. Secure it with a twist of thin wire allowing the fabric ends to swag freely. Don't worry about the raw edges because there are none ... remember it was a finished tablecloth. For the finishing touches, just tie a decorative tassel or accent cord around each end and cascade down over the top of the lace side jabots. Because this is a very lightweight decorating style, add tassels in a color that is close to the color of the lace – now is not the time to contrast with color.

Glass bottles and cork-lidded jars make great decorating accents. Simply add fresh carrots, string beans or other long skinny veggies to an empty bottle along with a few sprigs of fresh thyme and dill weed. Fill with apple cider vinegar (the dark brown color is the trick) and pop on the cork. Tie a big raffia bow around the throat and – WOW! – instant Country French accent pieces that look great displayed on your kitchen counter top!

For a really smashing bathroom, try painting the walls a deep rich color. Experiment with shades of orange-red or intense blue-greens. Colors like black-based greens, navy blues, or burgundies are rich colors but they are also **DARK** colors. Colors like this have a lot of black or umber in their pigmentation; thus not only are they deep and rich but primarily they are **DARK**. For this project, you want **DEEP** and rich color. Seek out the darkest shade of a bright color so that you'll end up with an intense deep glow on your walls and not a dated dark color scheme.

Next select a ceiling color about about 3 shades lighter than the walls. And don't forget the trim work; an off-white high gloss alkyd paint looks really fresh and clean against darker colored walls. For the vanity, try a shade lighter than the trim color. This will help to brighten the overall room, and **FORCE** you to clean out the vanity.

Now's the perfect time to get rid of the old shampoo bottles and other clutter hiding way in the back. You can't lose ... a new deep and rich look for the bathroom **PLUS** extra space - what are you waiting for?

Got a linen closet that's a time bomb waiting to explode? Why not treat the inside of a linen closet as if it were a decorative display shelf? It's easy. First drag out all of the debris, junk, out-of-date medicines, etc. Then remove the door and hinges and fill in the gaines (depressions in the trim work where the hardware was installed) with a good grade of wood putty.

After three coats of paint the color of the trim, you'll be surprised how the depressions seem to disappear into the overall casing as if a door was never installed. Next paint the interior walls **AND** ceiling several shades darker than the surrounding bath or hallway walls. Repaint the interior shelving so that it's fresh and free from sticky shelf paper.

Now, instead of throwing the stuff back into the closet, arrange all of the items in baskets, pots and decorative containers much like you would if this was a baker's rack in the middle of your living room. I like to store all of my medicines in small decorative boxes and baskets instead of just lining them up on the shelf.

As for the towels, make sure they're neatly folded or rolled and stacked by color. If the towels are nothing more than scraps, now's the time to replace those rags. Arrange each shelf so that it's interesting to look at while serving a purpose. Placing a large bowl of potpourri amongst the items is also a good idea plus a great way to permanently scent your bath linens.

The tall empty space below the last shelf is an ideal space for a large wicker or decorative metal laundry basket. Try to get something other than plastic so that in addition to being an accessible "target" for dirty towels, it will also be a finishing touch to your new linen display area.

Short on kitchen storage space? Use the empty wall space between the stove and exhaust hood for a pot rack. It's simple and inexpensive. Here's how: Mount a heavy-duty metal bath towel bar beneath the exhaust hood about 18" above the back of the stove. Remember, think safety - no plastic racks here - only use metal!

Now you can hang all of those pots and cooking utensils that were cluttering up your cabinets. To secure the pots, cut and bend wire clothes hangers to form inexpensive "s" hooks and simply place one end through the little hole found in the handles of each pot and cooking tool. CAUTION: Because of fire hazard, don't hang garlic strings or dried herbs with the pots and utensils.

To give a small room a real sense of comfort and style, try adding texture to the walls. Start by applying pre-mixed sheet rock mud to the existing wall. I like to use a heavy-duty bristle brush or round head white-wall tire brush; the bristles will leave the gooey mud with a nice lumpy texture. Let this air dry for about 15 minutes. Then, before it completely dries, take a long wallpaper squeegee and lightly pull down over the lumpy wall surface in a random pattern. This will give some areas a slick smooth surface while others will remain pitted and pock-marked. Once this dries for at least 24 hours, simply paint the textured walls with a good quality latex satin or semi-gloss paint.

Here's an instant decorating trick ... try adding 3 small pocket-size hardcover books to a low narrow rectangular shaped basket. Stand the small books up vertically, positioned in the center of the basket leaving plenty of room to one side. To the right of the books, tuck in a small artificial fern and on the left side of the books add a small bowl. Fill it with sweet-smelling potpourri and you've got a great dress-up for the back of the commode tank.

To spruce up your kitchen and keep the kids happy during meal time, try upholstering the chairs in vinyl flannel-backed tablecloths. Nowadays these easy-clean discount store tablecloths are more then just red and white check picnic cloths; some of the patterns are really **GREAT!** Start by centering the pattern on the face of the seat cushion. Next cut off the excess, just leaving enough to staple the cloth under the seat. **WOW!!** Instant decorating that's water and spill proof.

For those of you who love to decorate and collect live interior house plants, here's a great idea to save you steps on watering day **PLUS** make a great design statement. Using an oversized metal catering tray (available at most cookware specialty shops), position the tray on a chest or long bench close to a window. Pick up a bag of oversized aquarium rock gravel and pour the 1-2 inch size round rocks into the tray so that it fills the entire tray bottom.

Next, transplant your favorite plants into natural terra cotta pots of varying sizes and shapes and add these to the rock lined tray. Now for the creative part ... finding something that is about 6-8 inches tall and fat and squatty looking.

For my tray, I've used an 8 inch glass building block but you may want to consider an
antique what-not piece or even an old wooden
box. You decide ... it's your project!

Now, using your squatty piece, snuggly
position this "creative item" into the center of
the tray amongst the plant groupings and on
top of the rocks. Place your most treasured
plant specimen on top so that it stands out
proportionately against the other plant
heights. If your specimen plant is a tall orchid
and the other container plants are low-lying
ivies and African violets, the proportional balance of the tall orchid and the low remaining
plants will be "off" - so be sure to consider this
when selecting your specimen plant.

To complete this informal arrangement,
add two mismatched candle sticks with natural beeswax candles. See? It's easy to get creative with something you love once you realize
your own creativity!

Design Notes ...

_____

_____

_____

_____

_____

_____

_____

_____

_____

_____

_____

_____

_____

LET IT HAPPEN – You're not going to be creative UNTIL YOU REALIZE you already have that God-given ability.

chapter seven

PROFESSIONAL THOUGHTS
How to Think, Work and
Understand Like a Pro

*S*everal years ago, while presenting a hands-on
wallcovering program to a group of do-it-yourselfers, I
noticed a few folks who had developed that dreaded bane
of professional speakers ... the blank look. You know the
expression ... the face that shows only confusion and a
complete lack of understanding. While the majority of my
audience was really into the subject (and paste) at hand, it
bothered me that I'd lost the attention of a few folks. So I
did what any good teacher would do – I called on the most
confused-looking guy in the room. It turned out, he really *was* confused and actually lost! It seems that he only

wandered into our conference room looking for directions to his next seminar! Thankfully, he was not easily embarrassed and even managed to relate a tale about the time he and his now ex-wife tackled their own wallpaper project together. (See, I've always said that husbands and wives should *never* hang wallpaper together if they want to stay married!) Needless to say, after the laughter died down, I continued to seek a reason for the blank look on a few other faces. It turns out that even a subject as basic as wallcovering has it's own language used to describe the work and products at hand. Since I was addressing a group of homeowners interested in home repair and fix-up, I was assuming that my audience knew this "wallpaper talk". Was I ever wrong! The few "blank-look" guys hadn't a clue as to what I was talking about. It seems I had failed to understand that even a subject as basic as wallpaper can be confusing, and even a bit intimidating, if you don't understand the words and practices used to describe the task at hand.

So the lesson in this story is mine – whenever I present design, I need to keep in mind that my audience, readers and D-I-Y clients are all depending on me to keep it simple as well as informative – so that everyone can decorate and understand like a pro!

Many times, when you start thinking about a new construction, remodeling or decorating project, you are filled with so much fun, hope and anticipation for the final glorious results that you fail to see the forest for the trees. No matter how small the project and the direction we've planned for, we are convinced that what we are about to undertake is the *perfect* answer and set about to the exclusion of all other ideas. But sometimes we get stuck in our certainty. Maybe the lighting issues are not right and the whole look of the room is

> **The results of any project that has had the input of a professional designer will always be spectacular.**

thrown off but we can't figure out why. Or, as in most cases, the room or project is newly completed, but it still doesn't feel as comfortable as we had hoped ... even after spending all that money! What went wrong?

So instead of just throwing up our hands in frustration, some of us actually admit that we need a little help. Sometimes just seeking advice from a friend really does help; you know, having someone with whom you can bounce an idea around or discuss a trouble spot. And someone to remind you to not forget the photo trick – it's a great way to double check your finished project (chapter #4) as well as to see what needs to be changed and/or adjusted. And, if we have the means to seek professional design assistance, by all means go for it! But by all means, whenever you're "stuck" seek out advice – it's the best way for you to solve your own problem.

And as for decorating problems, the results of any project that has had the input of a professional designer will always be spectacular, especially if you, the prospective client, approach the relationship as one seeking a valued service. And it's this *service* that a professional contractor, interior designer, architect, or experienced decorator can and *will* provide if you *allow the relationship and creativity to be productive.*

Allow the relationship and creativity to be productive.

If you're having a hard time understanding this concept, consider what happened to me recently while I was auditioning for the host spot on a TV show. It was fun, exciting and just a touch nerve-wracking. Between takes and call backs, my mind started to wander on the similarities between my working with an unknown director for the first time and that of a client working with a designer.

Both situations are creative and demanding of trust. As an auditioning talent, I have no say in the final edited version of my work on tape. While before the camera, I have to rely blindly on the director's ability to get my lighting, placement, and editing cuts correct so that the end result comes across professionally and seemingly effortless

Trust takes a lot of courage.

– in other words, I'm relying on him 100% to make me and my talents look the best that they can be. So after a brief explanation and pre-tape demonstration, my meeting with the director is over and blind trust needs to kick in. I am totally in his hands. Even if I want to tell him how to position this camera or other tid-bits, I can't. For to do so would not only ruin my audition chances, but it would impugn his professionalism.

Trust of this kind – to totally rely on a person whom you've just met to make creative decisions on your behalf – takes a lot of courage. Could this be similar to the relationship between client and designer while working on a major construction or decorating project? We'll see.

Whenever a homeowner makes the decision to involve a professional designer in a construction/decorating project, there are numerous issues to discuss and deep-seated concerns to address – and there *should* be! It is the client's house and a lot of money is at stake, not to mention the client's comfort and well-being in her own home. So design-related questions and creativity concerns like these are common. "Will this new designer understand my wishes?" "Will she understand the building process completely so that the inevitable screw-ups and delays can be effectively handled in a professional and timely manner?"

Does the designer 'see' the end result in the same light as the client?

And most importantly, "Does the designer 'see' the end result in the same light as the client?" Sound like the same scenario as my audition? Wrong!

Unlike the audition, where my creativity concerns were discussed only briefly, in the professional designer/client working relationship, the client *must* express those fears, concerns and wishes during the first meeting at great length. Failing to do so will only lead to dissatisfaction, and in some cases, a waste of money. I like to think of it as a client's *responsibility* to bring these creativity concerns and other questions to the foreground during that first important meeting.

Halfway through the project is *not* the time to start to seek creativity changes and answers to those initial questions, especially when the project is already underway. To nit-pick the direction the professional has implemented is not fair to the designer or the client. Incessantly questioning tiny details or trying to micro-manage

> **Halfway through the project is NOT the time to start to seek creativity changes.**

the design project from the designer's back seat is a sure way to alienate the designer and doom the project. And the one to suffer the most will only be you, the client.

If you've decided to involve a design pro in your next project, consider it your responsibility to settle the creative issues up front and *let the professionals* do the job you've hired them to do! I know this is a hard concept to understand and even harder to carry out, but if you've elected to hire a professional in the design process, then you must heed this advice ... your future comfort – and bank balance – depend on it.

> **Let the professionals do the job you've hired them to do!**

$\mathcal{I}$t seems that every few weeks I'm asked the difference between a decorator and an interior designer. The answer is obvious to me, but the differences are still frequently misunderstood by the general public. I thought that a little "brain teaser" exercise would help clarify the two career paths.

The idea of turning creative control over to someone else is scary.

Consider the various professions listed below and mentally note the differences between the two career options within the fields listed.

Counselor	-	Psychiatrist
Stock Trader	-	Certified Financial Advisor
Cook	-	Registered Dietician
Optician	-	Ophthalmologist
LPN nurse	-	RN nurse
Decorator	-	Registered Interior Designer

During your reverie, I'm sure you'll notice that the professions in both columns perform the same functions some of the time even though their educational training is different. In other words, both career titles perform the same *basic* job but those listed on the right hand side do it with greater detail and expertise while also covering *more areas within that field.* Now, don't fall into the trap of thinking that the left side of the professional list seems to hold a lesser job classification – nothing could be further from the truth! Remember that *both* career paths are important and *necessary* so that the field itself will be viable and able to live up to the service it was designed to offer.

> Decorators and registered interior designers perform the same 'basic' job, but the designer does it with greater detail and expertise.

To further enhance your understanding between decorator and designer, here's a simple explanation to help avoid confusing the two careers:

- a *decorator* is someone who is very talented in arranging interior furnishings, accessories and selecting colors. No specific education or business credentials are required to establish a practice;

- a *registered interior designer* is a professionally schooled, educated and trained person who rearranges space within the walls of a building. Practicing in both residential (homes and houses) and contract (large offices, hospitals, stores, etc.) settings an interior designer also implements remodeling and construction projects, as well as specifies the materials necessary for project completion. In most states, a person holding and using the title of registered interior designer must also meet strict qualifications and have their practice regulated by the state's board of architects and engineers. In addition, he/she *also* arranges furnishings, accessories and selects colors – just like a decorator.

*T*he concept of turning creative control over to someone else is scary. Sometimes, however, you have to briefly relinquish control of the reins so that the horse can run a little down the path of creativity. Think of it this way; imagine you've hired a dressmaker to create a wedding gown from scratch. After lots of meetings, review of sketches, preliminary fittings and approvals of each detail you have given final approval and the last "go ahead". Would you now have the audacity to impugn their professionalism by insisting to watch them actually sew each stitch? It's one thing to insist on lots of fittings and be sure to be involved in every aspect of the creation of the dress, but to watch them sew each bead and seam? Of course not!

To do so would question their ability, and if nothing else, make them resent and dread your project so that the end result is barely within the expected level stated in the contract instead of the dazzling dress it could have been.

The same is true in the client/designer relationship for any major construction or decorating project. Before you end up dissatisfied and uncomfortable with your client/designer "creative" working relationship, here are a few points to consider:

- Ask *lots* of questions on the front end

- Express your tastes by using as many examples as possible –magazine photos, fabric swatches, etc.

- Express your distaste as well, so that your pro can see and understand what you *don't* want. Again, magazine photos are a great tool but sometimes it's easier to find pictures of rooms and styles that you find unappealing.

- Read and understand the contract completely – this is one case when it's OK to nit-pick. Do whatever you have to do, just be sure you know what you're signing and agreeing to. Remember, it's not the designer's fault if you've signed the contract without understanding it completely on the front end.

- Monitor the project carefully – it's your home and style so be sure to be actively involved and available to assist the designer whenever necessary.

After all, the finished project is supposed to look and feel like you and not just be another clone of the design pro. And then ... let the professional you've hired do the job you've hired them to do!

Looking for a professional designer
in your area? Call the worldwide **ASID**
referral line for a pro near you.
1-800-775-2743.

DESIGN BASICS ...

Wallpaper terms:

· Scrubbable: Any type of wallcovering that can be scrubbed with a soft-bristle brush and a prescribed detergent solution.

· Strippable: Wallcoverings that can be completely removed from walls without steaming or scraping.

· Paper-Backed Vinyl: A wallcovering that has a paper substrate laminated to a vinyl sheet (which is the ground). The ground for paper-backed vinyl makes up 25-50 percent of the total thickness.

· Fabric-Backed Vinyl: Wallcoverings that contain a solid vinyl intermediate layer laminated or coated to a woven or non-woven fabric substrate.

· Commercial (Contract): Wallcoverings that must meet certain minimum physical and performance characteristics, such as flammability, washability, scrubability, stain resistance, and tear strength, set by Federal guidelines. There are three classifications; Type I, Type II, and Type III.

· Documentary: Wallcovering that is copied from a historic wallcovering or fabric.

· Colorway: Combination of colors in a wallcovering pattern. Oftentimes, the same pattern is available in several colorways within a collection.

· Repeat: Vertical distance between identical points in a wallcovering pattern.

· Substrate: The backing of the wallcovering.

· Embossing: Raised effect created by impressing a texture onto wallcovering rather than printing it.

· Ground: The surface upon which the wallcovering pattern or decoration is printed.

If you are having trouble getting fresh paint to adhere to kitchen walls it's not the paint but how you **PREPARE** the walls. You'll first need to wash the walls and ceiling with a granulated cleaning powder in order to remove any cooking grease and cigarette smoke residue.

After this dries, apply one coat of a shellac-base sealer. I recommend the readily available **KILZ**. Remember to read the label for clean-up instructions because, unlike paint, turpentine and water is not used with this product.

Then paint with two coats of a latex enamel or alkyd semi-gloss. With all of the fumes you'll be generating, be sure to open the windows for plenty of fresh air in addition to turning on the air conditioner. And, if you're pregnant or have upper respiratory problems, **STAY OUT OF THE HOUSE** and let someone else do this job!

When using paint to update your home's exterior, be sure to consider the roof shingle color, brick color, stonework and any feature of the house that can't be changed. Since all of these architectural elements have color undertones, it's important to consider these natural colors **BEFORE** deciding on the final paint color palette. **EXAMPLE:** If the house has an orange brick foundation and a brown roof, a good trim color would be tan with a green or brown undertone. A lap siding color could be a darker shade of this same tan.

If you were to use a pink-based tan with the orange bricks and brown roof, then, when applied, this particular shade of tan paint would turn or "cast" a sickly shade of peach. This is called **REFLECTANCE** and most home-owners underplay its power. Simply put, light paint colors will pick up **ANY** and **ALL** of the other colors surrounding it, including existing colors found in bricks, stones, trees, etc. Also be sure to keep reflectance in mind as it **DRA-MATICALLY** affects the color white.

After you decide on the perfect color scheme, buy a quart of each color and sample the colors on large sections on each side of the house (since the natural light direction also has a bearing on the paint color). Now is the time to make any adjustments to the paint formula to reduce the amount of reflectance found with most light colors.

And be sure to keep in mind the paint trick of camouflage; if the house has an ugly detail or it's not architecturally important, paint that area the same color as the background. A good example are downspouts on a brick house. No need to accentuate these necessi-ties, so paint all of the vertical downspouts (the horizontal sections are called gutters and these should be painted the same color as the trim) a reddish color that closely approximates the natural brick color. I recommend using a latex flat so that the dull nature of the paint will blend better with the finish on the existing bricks.

When considering a kitchen remodel without enlarging your existing square footage, keep in mind the size requirements associated with a work island or countertop island. So before getting your heart set on an island, get out the tape measure and the masking tape for a little show and tell.

On the floor, measure and mark with the masking tape a minimum of 36" out remaining space (the largest area you can safely and effectively use for the location of the new work island). Keep in mind that unless you have an area remaining of at least 2 feet square, your remodel plans should not include an island. Also keep in mind that if the space in front of any appliance is also to be used as a traffic path or hall pass-through, then be sure to increase the distance from the island to the face of the appliance to at least 48".

This increase in clear square footage will allow for the extra floor space needed to get from one room to another while passing through the kitchen without having to squeeze by.

Countertop space - there never seems to be enough, especially when preparing family size meals! In your remodel plans, be sure to design at least 24" of countertop next to the sink. And don't forget the stove area; there should be at least 18" to one side and a minimum of 8" on the other. This extra work surface allows for any hot pots and other cooking utensils to be transferred safely from the stove to a safe holding area.

For added design savvy, try hanging an oversized decorative mirror overtop of the bathroom sink. The trick to making this work is in the lighting placement. Hire a licensed electrician to move the existing wall-mount light fixture over the vanity to a higher spot further up on the wall. The center of the electrical mounting box should be at least 84".

Once the light fixture is re-installed this higher location will enable you to hang a tall vertical mirror.

Aside from making your bath look great, a taller mirror is also a fantastic design trick to visually create more space in a tiny bath.

Having a hard time determining the amount of wall paint to buy? Here's a simple formula to determine the amount of paint you will need:

Keep in mind that paint is based on SUR-FACE square footage. To arrive at that magic number, you'll first have to determine the room perimeter or distance around the room on the floor. Simply measure the wall along the floor line and then multiply that number by the height of the wall. Next, subtract out 21 sq. ft. per door opening and 15 sq. ft. per window opening. Combine all of the totals together for the wall surface square footage of the entire room.

Since most paints cover 400 sq. ft. per gallon, just divide your wall surface total by 400 and round up to the next highest number.

If your walls will need two coats, just double this figure. To determine the surface square footage of the ceiling, just measure the length of the ceiling and multiply it by the width.

Here's an example: a room is 12' by 15' with an 8 ft. ceiling. It has 2 doors and 2 windows. The walls are to be painted in latex satin, the trim is alkyd semi-gloss and the ceiling will be latex flat.
Determine surface wall area:
54' (perimeter) x 8' (height) = 432 sq.ft.
Determine surface trim area:
42' (2 doors) + 30' (2 windows) = 72 sq.ft.
Subtract trim area from wall surface totals: 432 - 72 = 360 sq.ft.
Determine gallons needed:
360 x 2 (2 coats) = 720
divided by 400 = 1.33 rounded to 2 gallons.
Buy: 2 gallons of latex satin wall paint

Another trick used by professionals to give the appearance of added cost and luxury is the aftercare given to fabrics once they are hanging. All the pros use a hand-held steamer to set the pleats or creases. Using a typical electric steam iron will only press already stiff fabric into hard knife-edged pleats, making the draperies hang like bands of corrugated cardboard. They also allow plenty of time for the fabric panels and top treatments to "relax". This part is simple - just pull the new panels so that they completely cover the windows for about 24 hours. This will ensure that all of the major wrinkles will fall out. For those stubborn creases, use the steamer until the fabric is moist. When it dries, the wrinkles will be gone.

For a really smashing room arrangement try the minimalist approach. Start by cleaning out your den - I mean **EVERYTHING!** So get ready to strip it clean. Now, only bring back into the room those items that are in **GREAT** shape and currently in fashion - everything else needs to be scheduled for a yard sale.

Next arrange what's left - hopefully the major furniture pieces - in a way totally new to the room. Now is the time to experiment and get creative with seating groupings. Remember that it's okay to be different with your arrangements - the minimalist approach to decorating with a comfortable twist!

When hanging family photos, framed pic-tures and artwork, be sure to remember your high school geometry. For a really interesting arrangement, try to balance the frames as if they were forming large rectangles, triangles and squares. Since this tip is so dependent on visual help, the only way I have to make sure you're really "getting" this point is to suggest you purchase my video, **MAKING THE MOST OF YOUR SPACE**. In the 45 minute video, I demonstrate this tip so that you'll instantly be able to hang, arrange and organize any and **ALL** of your treasured items on the walls. Other areas covered in my tape are numerous tips that prove to be helpful throughout the home. To order this tape or the entire decorating video series, please call **1-800-265-2992**.

Design Notes ...

_____

_____

_____

_____

_____

_____

_____

_____

_____

_____

_____

_____

_____

_____

Why seek professional advice?
Because it is a service that has both
monetary and emotional value.

chapter eight

PLAN TO KEEP IT COMFORTABLE
The Bottom Line of Decorating Success

My dog, cute as he may be, *stinks*! Sorry, Kelsey Rufus, but ever since we started growing your hair for that grooming competition, you shed like crazy and the aroma coming from your little body is *phew*!

Normally, my show cocker spaniel Kelsey Rufus is professionally groomed and bathed every few weeks so that he's always presentable and a joy to behold. But since he's been entered in a national grooming competition, we've had to allow his coat to become overly long and unkempt so that during the actual event the groomer can

transform him back to his beautiful self in record time –
whatever possessed me to agree to this? So what is the
relationship between my cocker's coat and decorating a
room?

Well, it got me thinking about how easy it is for
something so pretty to quickly become a detriment to my
comfort. Confused?
Consider this. When
we first decorate, add
a new sofa, or freshen
up a room, the entire
space seems to glow
and we feel fantastic
within that area of our

> **It's the nature of the
> universe that every
> item has a place AND
> reason within the space
> to which it's assigned.**

homes. The new fabrics, carpeting and other design elements all contribute to make the space one of overwhelming comfort and beauty. But as time goes by and life gets
in the way, we all slip in the maintenance department.

When it was freshly "done" we were ever so con-
scious of misplaced items within that new space – stray
sneakers, newspapers, and rumpled cushions would
never be found scattered about our newly decorated room.

But after a while, we become blinded to the disarray that causes our homes to look and *feel* dirty. It's as if we don't even see the dirt and disarray. It just happens. And it's unfortunate because our homes are not meant to be boxes of chaos and clutter.

So just like Kelsey Rufus, who's not supposed to have hair in overlong lengths, our homes are not meant to be unkempt and in a constant state of disarray. When that happens, our comfort is compromised. Remember that it's the nature of the universe that every item has a place *and* reason within the space to which it's assigned. And dust balls the size of cats just don't fit the bill – especially in a space that was once so beautiful. So, the bottom line of any decorating project is the ongoing maintenance required for keeping it beautiful, comfortable and attractive. Otherwise, it *will* stink – just like Kelsey Rufus. In plain words, to keep your house comfortable, get rid of *anything* that doesn't belong and your house will amazingly seem refreshed, revitalized, and once again newly decorated – giving you that wonderful feeling of comfort.

*E*very Autumn, just in time for the kids to be back in school while the trees are starting to turn bold colors, most women seem to turn their attention to decorating. It seems that everyone wants to spruce up their homes for the upcoming holidays and those long periods of time spent indoors during the colder weather. It's as if everyone gets the seasonal "decorating flu" or a bad case of the "fix-ups."

And it's a frustrating time - all of the Fall activities, plus this overwhelming desire to decorate. I can't explain it, but every woman I know gets this way during the transitional months of the year. Maybe it's in our genes, our personality or our need to be in charge. Whatever it is, we all want to change by decorating in the fall of the year.

> **Everyone wants to spruce up their homes for the upcoming holidays.**

In most homes, there are so many areas to work on, from carpeting to paint to window treatments and accessories, that a starting point is hard to determine. With so many areas to try out those new decorating tips, it's almost impossible to decide which project to tackle first.

> **Without a planned outline or list of things that need fixing up, you're just blowing in the wind.**

Well, for those of you who've seen my many TV decorating segments, I'm sure you'll recognize this phrase ... *don't do anything until you have an overall plan!!*

I know I've said it hundreds of times, but this advice is *really* important; without a planned outline or list of things that need fixing up, including the projected costs, you're just blowing in the wind. So keep in mind that any time you start to instigate change – and even a small fix-up project is *change* – you've entered into a process of flux that will affect all the other areas of the room or house. Always remember that in decorating, every action produces a reaction that demands decorative attention.

Let's stop and think about that for a moment. Say you were to change your hair color. Imagine you are currently a natural milk-chocolate brunette with long straight hair. You are also 15 pounds overweight. So you decide to "fix up" yourself and lose those pounds, cut and re-style your hair, and change the overall color from brown to red. All of this is wonderful – but unless you plan for other changes that *will* occur because of these personal *fix-ups*, your life will be a mess. Unless you address the dilemma of your old clothes not being the "right" look for your new hair style and color, or even the wrong size for the new slimmer *you*, all of your efforts to change will be wasted because nothing will look or fit right.

> **In decorating, every action produces a reaction that demands decorative attention.**

Decorating or sprucing up a home produces those same type of chain reactions if you don't plan for those inevitable changes that *will* occur once you complete your project. In other words, once you change something in a room, it affects *everything* in that room. Just by simply updating the bedside lamps, all of the other lamps within the room become dated and worn looking ... the list goes on. The hard part is recognizing this fact and then planning to address those other areas so that the entire room will look fresh and comfortable without having to change everything in the entire room *all* at the same time!

Remember that if there are areas not to be considered for redecoration, you had better modify your new spruce-up plan to allow for this lack of decorating activity throughout the rest of the room, otherwise the entire room will always appear to be wearing a size 14 dress over a size 8 figure. If this analogy has you lost, consider this decorating dilemma: haven't you ever walked into a neighbor's house to admire the new sofa and thought to yourself, "HMMMM, looks nice, but what about the rest of the room?" Worse yet, this thought might have crossed your mind ... "They've spent all that money on new curtains and the place still looks the same!"

> **Plan to address [all] areas so that the entire room will look fresh and comfortable.**

You get the picture, and, I hope, the intent of this chapter. You can't begin a change without first having given some thought to the effect it will have on the rest of the decorating within that space. So if you think that by spending thousands of dollars on a new window treatment it will make the overall room look and feel better, *think again*! Sure, the new window treatment will enhance the window, but if the sofa still has rips and the walls are spotty with finger prints, or the carpet is an outdated off white, than all of those hard-earned dollars you've just spent on the new window treatment will go wasted. A better use of your dollars and decorating efforts would be to scale back on the cost of the windows and pay some attention to the sofa and walls.

> You can't begin a change without first having given some thought to the effect it will have.

But you really *liked* those $$ window treatments! Well, instead of getting frustrated and then doing nothing, you can start to change your entire room with a plan. I mean a real decorating detail plan ... one that includes paint chips of the new wall color, fabric samples of the new furniture, photos of the accessories and everything that will eventually fill the space, and so on. In other words, complete the space *on paper* as if you could begin and finish the project in a "soup to nuts" fashion all in one fell swoop! The hard part is to always keep this plan handy so that it can remind you on a regular basis that sooner or later the room will "come together" and be finished. And the amazing part is that, once on paper, it *will* get finished!

To make the creation of the plan easy, be sure to glue all of the samples, paint chips and other decorating wish-lists on a large board so it serves as a reminder of what's to be. I like to keep the planning board handy – like on top of the mantel or tacked to the wall – so that *anyone*, including yourself, who walks into that room proposed for change can immediately see the direction that space will take.

> **"Keep it clean to keep it new."**
> **– Deborah Burnett**

Another benefit of the planning board is that its mere presence gives one hope that the project will eventu-

"The wise woman builds her house, but the foolish one pulls it down with her own hands."

— Proverbs

ally end and the entire room will be complete. So even if you're on a tight budget and the plan won't be affordable for a few years, the planning board still gives you something to look forward to. After all, isn't that half the fun of decorating?

*I*n addition to a good weekly general cleaning, here are a few other areas that also need attention in order to get our houses back into that comfortable place we call home:

- Inspect all sofa and chair cushions for droopy foam, stained fabrics, worn welts, etc. It's not that costly to repair / replace these items, and what a difference it makes to the overall appearance of the room! Remember, only English castles look fashionable with worn upholstery and mushy cushions.

- Deep-clean your light fixtures, shades and chandeliers. Did you know that almost 20% of our household lighting can be lost due to dust? For oversize crystal chandeliers, simply hang an open umbrella from the bottom of the fixture and then spray glass cleaner until it drips from every crystal fob and pendant. When it's dry, get out the sunglasses WOW – what a sparkle!

- Roll back all area rugs and vacuum the under-layment and pads. Did you know that most household allergens can be traced to dander,

mites, and just plain dirt infesting the underside of carpeting? To make matters worse,
these critters stink. All you have to do to get a
full whiff is just walk into a vacant house where
the central HVAC has been turned off for a few
days!

• Actively scrub every shower stall, glass door
  and tile wall within a bathroom. It takes more
  than an occasional swipe with the spray cleaner to get the job done due to the soap build-up
  and airborne steam distributing those same
  soap particles throughout the room. You'll be
  amazed at the sense of increased space when
  mirrors, glass doors and slick walls are shiny
  clean.

• Get tough and throw out dying and leggy-look-
  ing plants. Come on, they won't come back to
  haunt you ... just put them outside behind the
  trash cans and let MS. NATURE take care of
  them. Still having a hard time? Just think back
  ... when was the last time you saw a magazine
  layout with plants that looked like the ones filling your living room or kitchen window sill?

To get additional ideas on how to develop
your creativity, send a self-addressed
stamped envelope and ask for the
"Creative Skill" checklist.

DESIGN BASICS ...

Countertop heights of 36" are usually standard in a kitchen, but if you are elderly or physically challenged, these standards are not for you. Just think how uncomfortable or totally useless a 36" tall cooktop would be if you were trying to fry bacon while seated in a wheelchair. But don't give up the independence or the fry pan just yet. Simply by lowering the countertop height, removing the cabinet underneath and installing a smooth surface cooktop, most challenged folks can begin to burn food just like the rest of us!

Forget all the layout basics you've ever heard! You know, the ones that say every house has to have a dining room, or every house has to have a formal living room. That was okay for the '40s lifestyle but it's a new millennium. How many folks do you **REALLY** know that use their dining table more than 3 times per year? Sure, a handsome dining table with accessory side pieces are nice and really handy during the holiday season. But if you're short on floor space, why waste that precious square footage with a large and formal dining room?

Instead, why not turn that little-used dining room into a small den or private sitting room? The small space is usually perfect for a couple of comfy club chairs with ottoman and a good size TV ... a perfect spot to unwind and relax for just the two of you! As for that formal living room, why not make it into a real **FAMILY** living **ROOM**? That's right, take the den sofa, chairs and large entertainment system and arrange the room so that the entire family has space enough to spread out and enjoy each other as well as watch TV in comfortable style. With a little planning and design savvy, even your old den furniture can look great and be presentable for company!

Nine-foot ceilings are a great design feature **IF** you know how to work with the space. Be sure to raise everything by at least 2 inches - chair rails, backs of sofas, heights of beds, etc.   Here's your chance to really use all of those handsome new oversized pieces and large scale accessories in 9 and 10 foot ceiling spaces.

Rethink the lighting. Change out those old cool white fluorescent tubes and replace them with the more energy efficient 3000 Kelvin ultralumes.

They will give the basement a warm pleasant feeling similar to regular 100 watt light bulbs, without making everyone's face look green as with standard fluorescent tubes.

Add several runs of incandescent track lighting around the perimeter of the room. For basement ceiling heights under 8', mount the tracks at a correct 60 degree angle. I recommend the smaller size head for most basements, one that will accept the R20 50 watt bulb. Since the new EPA law has gone into effect that will phase out the R20 lightbulbs, you may want to purchase track heads, which will also accept the new ER20 size bulb. And don't forget to add plenty of table and accent lamps scattered throughout the room. Apothecary and torchier-styled lamps really help to brighten a room without adding much design impact or cost; they just seem to blend into the beautifully lit background.

Still looking for another way to brighten the basement living area? Simply position oversize containers filled with beautiful show plants (NOT the half-dead leftovers from summer!) and add upright light cans behind each container using a "Dawn's Pink" bulb.

Consider a color change for the ceiling of the porch to a paler version of the house trim color. Or be daring and paint the ceiling a pale turquoise or blue. It makes the area much more inviting and pleasant.

Painting the front door a bold color is a great way to establish your personal style. Be sure to prep the surface properly and use an oil base gloss paint; you'll be pleased with the results!

Add a decorative accent piece to the sidewalk or propped near the front door. A rustic wagon filled with seasonal potted plants and flowers works well on the front porch of a home that is decorated in a warm and comfortable style.

Casement-style windows (long windows without grids which crank open on side hinges) are not suited for shutter accent because they are too contemporary in overall styling. The same goes for Jalousie or Florida- style windows.

Can you place shutters on the back of the house? Well, if the window size fits, and the house would look better with shutters on the back or all four sides, then GO for it!

When shopping for tools, keep comfort in mind. If it feels good in your hand, buy it. Just because most men's toolboxes have large-headed nails and heavy claw hammers doesn't mean that we need these in our tool baskets. I find that a small lightweight hammer and a few finishing nails without heads are all I need for this department. The same goes for saws.

A small hand-held hack saw is sufficient for most projects; for anything larger get the lumberyard to cut it for you.

Whenever cleaning and running the vacuum cleaner be aware of the damage you can cause to your fine decorative floor items. A good oriental or bound area rug should never have the beater bar of the electric vacuum run over it; the vacuum will "eat" the binding tape and cause the rug to unravel. Instead use a good broom to sweep the dirt off the rug perimeter and fringe and then just use the electric vacuum in the direct center of the rug.

Tip for polishing silver: instead of using commercial cleaning polishes, use a white paste of baking soda and water. This will help our silver stay bright and shiny. Remember that anything that touches the silver surface will eventually leave a tarnish mark. This includes your rubber gloves. These usually contain sulfur which accelerates the tarnish process, so do yourself a favor - only use cotton gloves whenever cleaning the silver.

For wooden front doors, don't forget the sun. That's right - that huge heat ball is very damaging to your front entryway. The sun literally bakes the clear finish and warps the wooden surface right off of your expensive door. To help keep the finish in a protective state, be sure to apply at least one coat of clear polyurethane every spring and fall.

A good general cleaning works wonders to improve the looks and you'll be able to see if any element is in need of painting or repair. Don't forget to prune shrubs and tree limbs that are blocking the front entry. A small amount of new mulch around the front shrubs will go a long way in your home's appearance and be easy on the pocketbook.

Glue guns are the best invention of the 20th Century! Be sure to keep plenty of extra glue sticks, since this is the one tool used most by women. With specialty caulk glue sticks, you can seal around the bathtub and shower stall. The specialty wood glue sticks do wonders securing broken furniture and the plastic glue sticks are a must for fixing children's toys. As a safety tip, be sure to keep a fireproof dish in the toolbox to act as a stand for the hot glue gun - they get extremely hot!

Design Notes ...

_____

_____

_____

_____

_____

_____

_____

_____

_____

_____

_____

_____

In design, you can solve a decorating problem in one of 2 ways: CAMOUFLAGE IT or ACCENTUATE IT so that it appears that THAT'S what you intended to do in the first place!

LESS IS MORE
Decorating With a Light Hand

$\mathcal{I}$ can't begin to count the times I am asked the question, "What's new in design?" And every time the answer is the same ... "NOTHING!" That's right, nothing is new in the field of design. It's just the same old stuff with a new twist. AND, if you wait long enough, what's old and 20 years out of date *will* come back again proclaiming to be the "new" trend in decorating – go figure!

Why is that? Well, the answer is simple. Whenever you're dealing with human comfort levels, and face it, that's what decorating is ... a way to make our lives more comfortable and pleasing, we as a species tend to fall back

on the tried and true. And what better way to be comfortable than to revert back to what has been a proven track
record for comfort?

What does all this mean? Get ready to never say
never – especially when it comes to shag carpeting,
chrome furnishings, colored glass decorative accents, and
other such items from the fifties and sixties. Before you
panic over poodle skirts with psychedelic flair, remember
my first statement, "Nothing is new in design, it's just the
same old stuff with a new twist!" So what is the so-called
new twist here? Professionally specified color and decorating restraint. That's right, those elements reflective of
'50s and '60s style that
were so horrible to
those of us who actu-
ally lived through the
first go around are
now tempered with a
restraint pleasing to
today's homeowner.
And those irritating
bright and glowing orange, neon yellows and impact lime
greens so popular in '60s home fashion are now toned

> If you wait long enough,
> what's old will come
> back again
> claiming to be 'new'.

down to pleasing pastel ranges that even Martha herself would approve.

For those of you who watch her show, I challenge you to look at the show's set accessories and overall design layout. I mean *really* look at the background "eye candy". It's all stuff from the middle decades, including the cabinet styling, dishware and even the storage prop baskets – the entire set is 1958. Watching that show, it's as if we're going back to the future and everything past is new again – only this time with more pleasing results.

*T*he other evening I experienced something rare ... a really good movie! It was a first-run feature film starring a well-known actor in a true story about a rather unorthodox doctor in the 1950s. Aside from the great story, there was something that impressed me greatly about this film - it's directorial subtlety. Even though this film dealt on a secondary level with the effects of childhood sexual abuse and a senseless murder - suicide, it did so without gratuitous violence or gory recreation of the events. It was so refreshing to see something truly sad without first "seeing" it through a movie-goers frightened eyes as the events are bloodily reenacted before our eyes. It was evident that this film director subscribed to that age-old adage of *less is more*.

> **It's as if we're going back to the future and everything past is new again – only this time with more pleasing results.**

Okay, so what's the tie-in to decorating? Well, that same old saying of "less is more" applies on an even greater scale to decorating our homes. Within the past few years, I've noticed a *more is not enough* trend by homeowners who decorate their homes without professional skill. It seems that if there is a product, style or pattern that they like, it's used *repeatedly* throughout the entire house. I was in one woman's living room the other day and I couldn't even sit down on the sofa. There were so many

> "One day an army of grey-haired women may quietly take over the earth."
> – Gloria Steinem

matched throw pillows, seat cushions and stuffed mementos that I was afraid I'd sink into the stuffing if I *did* sit down. It was too much. Obviously, she loved to decorate without knowing how to make it attractive or comfortable.

To further explain this "more is not enough" disease, I'm sure you've been noticing the recent explosion of magazine ads for local furniture stores, wallpaper collections, bed linens and antique accessory shops. Talk about clutter! It seems that every piece that's featured in the store is displayed in the ad. I recall examining one such linen ad for several minutes before I was even able to figure out what the product was that the ad was trying to sell; there was so much stuff on the unmade looking bed that I couldn't even see the sheets the copy was referring to.

The sheet pattern was great; crisp green leaves against the stark white background was classic. But in this advertisement, that same pattern was repeated in *everything* ... the sheets, bedspread, window treatments, throw pillows, wallpaper, area rugs, lamp shades, wallpaper border, book jackets, bath towel edge trim and even the ceramic accessories! All the surfaces in this one room were covered in this same pattern. Repeated over and over again, the pattern was almost psychedelic and the ad unreadable.

> **"The mark of the immature man is that he wants to die nobly for a cause, while the mark of a mature man is that he wants to live humbly for one."**
> **– J.D. Salinger**

Unfortunately this *"more is not enough"* and *"too much is great"* style of decorating is becoming the norm. It seems that all across America folks without professional skills are filling their homes with an overabundance of "matching stuff." And the irony is that the homeowners who actually live in these homes can't understand why their house "just doesn't feel right!" They wonder why their homes are not comfortable.

It seems that all across America we're filling our homes with an over-abundance of "matching stuff".

With that in mind, take some time to re-examine your decorating style and be on the lookout for this "more is not enough" trend. It can show up in the bedroom that you share with your husband: too many floral pillows, laced-edged fabrics everywhere, dried flower arrangements on every surface, and stuffed animals galore. It can also be found in the kitchen with too many decorative accessories that don't allow for any clear space on the countertop. Keep in mind that *empty* is okay. You don't have to fill *every* corner and every surface to have a wonderfully decorated and comfortable home. A professional skill to keep in mind is that it's okay to have nothing – empty space is good.

So what is the answer to the "more is not enough" approach in decorating? By seeking ideas from the past, with the professional skill of a light decorating touch, the subtle approach to displaying or telling anything worthwhile is always perfected with restraint. Keep in mind that it's not always necessary to beat someone over the head with an overabundance of information, decoration or fake re-creation for them to get the point. Whether it's a movie or a decorating project, subtlety and restraint are key to making the experience truly rewarding and comfortable.

> **Empty is okay. You don't have to fill every corner and every surface to have a wonderfully decorated and comfortable home.**

With that in mind, the next time you really fall in favor with a certain decorative pattern, or new trendy color, or current "hot" theme – don't abuse it. Re-

> **Subtlety and restraint are key to making the experience truly rewarding and comfortable.**

member that *restraint* in using that favored decoration will go a long way in creating a truly comfortable home – one that you and all of the family can enjoy.

$\mathcal{W}$ant to find out "What's New" and coming down the decorating pike? Check out the upcoming future "past" decorating trends by:

- Examining the ages of today's disposable income group. Those folks with the most amount of $$$ to spend on non-essential items are all products of the '50s. And it's those baby-boomers who are now controlling the home fashion direction back to the past ... only this time with a little more restraint in color, flair and style. It's their influences that are affecting the home fashions for all age groups. To see what I'm talking about, keep a notebook handy while you're watching your favorite TV show, scanning through women's magazines or just walking around the local shopping mall – you'll be amazed to see all of the "new" deco- rating products that resemble the past.

- Notice TV news reports for a reoccurring theme. Stories about wars, famine and other such horrors usually tend to put a damper on our more widely creative efforts and result in neutral colors and dull textural finishes, while ongoing articles about the environment and global conditions result in our use of greens and other natural colors. For these outside influences to affect our decorating trends, usually a period of at least one year must pass before we'll start to see the effects.

- Take a walk down the plastic goods section of the local discount store. The colors you'll see displayed on the shelves are the true reflection of what your neighbors are buying and how they're decorating their homes.

DESIGN BASICS ...

Paint tips: For walls always insist on a good quality latex acrylic paint. For durability and clean-ability I recommend the new latex satin finishes - not too shiny but just enough to scrub up without leaving streaks. Ceilings are the place to save a few dollars, so purchase a low grade of latex flat. And since the trim is where all the action is, go for the gold. The high cost of a gallon of top quality alkyd semi - gloss is worth the steep price the first time you try to clean up with a scrub brush - the paint will still be there no matter what brush you use! For other areas with wood, such as doors, cabinets and shelving, use only alkyd or oil based paints - the extra protection given by oil based paints is well worth extra cost and painting labor.

The use of primary pigment colors such as bright red, yellow, and bold blue are a great **ACCENT** color for the nursery. They work well as colors for wall hangings, bedding, lamps and rugs. As wall or ceiling colors, they prove to be too stimulating for the human eye to be peac-ful, especially when used in large amounts in a small room. Instead, try using pale tints of

lavenders or blue-green colors as wall colors
and even a paler tint of blue for the ceiling.

Designing a child's nursery can be tricky
unless you follow these basics: Keep in mind
that most children will occupy the original
nursery for at least 4 years, so it's a good idea
to design with the child's height in mind. This
means placing borders and custom stenciling
at 35-37 inches in the room. Trying to go to
sleep? Be sure to cover the windows with a
room darkening treatment; a simple throw
treatment looks great but don't forget to
install blinds or shades for light control and
contrast.

When collecting tools and utensils for the
home "toolbox", don't forget the pliers and
nippers. These come in all sizes and shapes.
The ones I use the most are the needle nose
and the 8" clipper / pliers combination. These
are a must if you do floral arrangements. You
can pull, twist and cut wire all with the same
tool; what a great idea! Another "must" is a

can of **WD40**. This stuff is the answer for anything that sticks - plus it's great for hiding
scratches on plastic countertops.

For the latest predictions in home fashion
color trends, check out the decorating magazines. For the lowdown on the colors that are
actually "selling" in the exact shades that
you'll see in real-life homes, be sure to spend
some time in the discount stores. Because of
the high volume of merchandise moved each
month by these merchants, they have a continual finger on the pulse of America's buying
habits and are able to successfully stock their
shelves with the everyday goods that folks are
demanding in the colors that they can use.

If you're stuck with an ugly chain link yard
fence, why not camouflage it? Here's how:
start by selecting a dull greenish-brown latex
flat paint. I recommend **Sherwin Williams
#2091**. Then, using a large lambswool nap
roller, apply one coat of this natural camouflage color. Don't worry about priming or even
covering the fence with a second coat - all

you're trying to do is eliminate the ugly galva-
nized color and have the fence disappear into
the surrounding background. A quick coat of
this color will do the trick nicely!

For a quick kitchen spruce-up that will complement any cabinet style and wood tone, try
the color green. A really pale shade of blue-
green on the ceiling is a wonderful pick-me-up
in the morning. For an afternoon boost, a
dusty mid-tone shade of grey-green is a wonderful contrast to the ceiling and blends well
with any natural wood tone color. And to top
it all off, paint the trim with a pastel tinted off-
white with a green cast. See? It's easy to "go
green", especially when you tie the whole room
together with a crisp blue- green window treatment.

When selecting paint colors from those
micro-mini paint samples provided by the manufacturers, keep this in mind. ALL paint samples are only approximated versions of what
the paint will look like on your walls, so be sure

to allow for a change once applied to the wall surface. Remember that a good thumb-rule of decorating know-how is to select your favorite color and then buy the next darker shade.

Design Notes ...

_____

_____

_____

_____

_____

_____

_____

_____

_____

_____

_____

_____

_____

_____

_____

_____

_____

_____

_____

_____

_____

_____

_____

_____

_____

When decorating a room, remember that **NOTHING** is better than the wrong something. It's better to have a completely **EMPTY** room than to have a space filled with decorating placeholders.

DEBORAH BURNETT, ASID

Deborah has many professional skills and talents to her credit. Additionally, she is a recognized:

- **Registered interior designer**
- **Licensed contractor**
- **Historic zoning commissioner**
- **FENG SHUI professional consultant**
- **American Society of Interior Designers award winner**
- **Newspaper columnist**
- **National TV design expert**
- **DAN RIVER national spokesperson**
- **Professional speaker & NSA member**

In addition to Deborah's many professional successes, she has been happily married to Louis for 25 years and is the proud mother of their son, Matt. When not busily at work, Deborah has found enjoyment puttering in her small greenhouse or skiing down mountainsides in Utah. Living in Springfield, Tennessee in a home that she and her husband designed, life is – *comfortable.*

To contact Deborah for product endorsements, speaking engagements, or professional design consultations, check out her web site at *www.deborahburnett.com* or call her offices during normal business hours: (615) 384-8337.

Dear Reader,

I hope that you've enjoyed learning
about the elements of design.
Hopefully, it will travel with you
from house to home throughout
your life. We all want our homes,
our work, and our lives to be rich
with comfort. Since the meaning
of the word "comfort" is as
diverse as our personalities, you
must set about discovering your
own unique definition.
I wish you the greatest
success in that effort,
and I'd be delighted
to hear from you
along the way.
Keep in touch!

How many others do you know who might benefit from the ideas and information to be found in *Comfortable Living by Design?* Show someone you care. It's a gift to be treasured and appreciated.

Also available is a hands-on decorating video series – *You Can DO IT!* – which teaches you how to achieve professional results throughout every room of your home. By using existing home decor and low-cost items commonly found in discount stores, Deborah shares her professional trade secrets to make your home more attractive and comfortable – affordably! Throughout each 45 minute tape, Deborah teaches you how to decorate like a pro by offering practical tips on:
- hanging and arranging pictures
- painting paneling
- furniture placement for small rooms
- home office set-up
- bath and kitchen spruce-ups
- and many more ...

If you're unable to find additional copies of *Comfortable Living by Design* at your local book store or would like to order Deborah's video series, use the order form below.

Please send me:

____ copies of **Comfortable Living by Design** (book)
____ copies of **Making the Most of Your Space** (video)
____ copies of **Make Overs for Less** (video)
____ copies of **Making Room for Children** (video)
____ sets of all 3 videos - SPECIAL OFFER $30.00 per set

____ items @ $14.95 each = _____
____ sets @ $30.00 each = _____
TN residents add 8.25% tax = _____
shipping/handling @ $2.50 each = _____
Total = _____

Ship to:

Name _____

Address _____

City _____ State ____ Zip _____

Phone (____) _____

Enclose a check made payable to Humble Abundance Publishers for your order and mail to:
Humble Abundance Publishers
140 Old Kinneys School Road, Springfield, TN 37172

To pay by credit card (Visa or Mastercard) call (800) 265-2992
Or fax order to: (615) 384-1137